Arou ~~World In 67

CW01468298

Michael Flynn

Copyright © 2023
All rights reserved

Dedication

In memory of Mum & Dad. Thank you for everything.

Acknowledgements

I'm grateful to everyone who has bought this book, thereby contributing to the Alzheimer's society's excellent work.

If you wish to donate further to the Alzheimer's society – please go to:

https://www.justgiving.com/fundraising/MelbaFlynn

Thanks to both my sisters; Natalie Jane, for all her unselfish caring and being there for both Mum & Dad in their final years; and Vanessa Louise, for being a wonderful host, as you will read about, for part of their World trip; and to both, for furnishing me with the details I forgot...or never knew, and some photographs.

Finally, I wouldn't have enjoyed the editing of this book so much were it not for the laughter from sharing anecdotes and explanations of their grandparents' travels to my wonderful children, Joe & Katie...as well as Katie's ability to decipher most of her grandad's writing!

About the Author

Melba & Raymond Flynn.

Edited by Michael Flynn

Having worked all their lives, bringing up three children, Melba & Raymond Flynn embarked on an 'around the world' trip, keeping a diary/log of every day of their adventure together. On finding the handwritten notebook, their son, Michael, decided to publish it and share their journey with those that knew this wonderful couple and others who simply love travelling…and to those whom it may inspire to see more of the world themselves!

Michael Flynn lives in London, where he is currently studying Archaeology. He has won numerous awards for Sports Sponsorship and was North West Entrepreneur of the Year in 2014. He is the founder, chairman, and non-exec director of various sports, health, and digital businesses.

Introduction

It wasn't an attempt to better Phileas and Passepartout's 80 days; it just ended up being 67 days for Mum & Dad to travel around the world, seeing some wonderful places, and meeting their daughter, Vanessa, and family in Australia for Christmas. Vanessa is child number 3 of 3, Natalie number 2, and me, their firstborn, Michael. We were all born in the sixties.

Mum and Dad, A.K.A. Melba Walker and Raymond Flynn, met in 1957 at the Sale Locarno, a dance hall on Washway Road, Sale, near Manchester, and they married in Cheadle, near Manchester, on 3rd September 1960.

So how did this book come about?

Well, on moving into my new house in London last year, I came across a ring file notebook with the title '1998/99 ROUND WORLD TRIP LOG' written in Dad's handwriting across the front. Dad had given this to me years before, which I'd put aside to read 'one day'. It was effectively Mum & Dad's logbook of their travels around the world that they embarked on three years after Dad retired early from his work. That 'one day' came a few months ago, so I decided to publish their travels in their very own words for friends, family, and anyone interested in an around-the-world adventure!

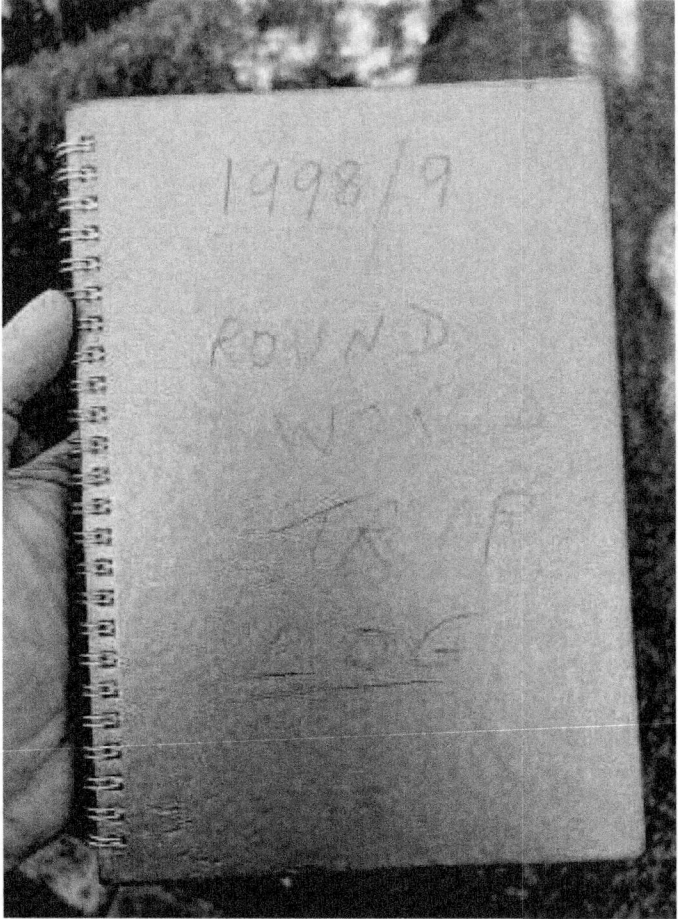

A bit about Melba and Raymond first.

Melba Kay Walker was born on 23rd January, 1936. She was born and lived at 12 Fencegate Avenue in Heaton Chapel, South Manchester. At Avondale school, Stockport, she was either top or second in her class at almost everything (I managed to see a few of her school reports when I was helping with her Mum's funeral). She was also, like her two sisters, very athletic and used to run for Sale Harriers. I'm without doubt that if Mum had been born 30 years or so later, she would have excelled at university and would likely have become a successful business leader. She had all the key attributes needed, very intelligent, great with people, and lots of empathy; as it was, back in those days, there was virtually no chance of women either going to university or a high-flying business career.

Using my maternal haplogroup information from my own mitochondrial DNA analysis that I've recently been analysing, I now know Mum came from the haplogroup H7, which is present in both Europe and West Asia. Her maternal line goes right back to a woman who lived approximately 9000 years ago, whose descendants migrated into Europe and into the Middle East. Her specific subgroup is present in Ashkenazi Jews, Romanians, Sardinians, and many Dutch people. She was also of the same ancestral line as Marie Antionette (which may explain the social lives of myself and both my sisters!).

Raymond Joseph Flynn was born on 15th August, 1936, at Beech Mount Maternity Home, North Manchester. He lived at 225 Woodlands Road, Crumpsall in North Manchester, and for a while, went to Xaverian College, Longsight, Manchester, until he finally snapped after months of being picked on by a particular 'Brother'/Monk; he punched him straight in the face, knocking him out with the one strike, and was immediately expelled. He continued his studies at the Manchester Central Library (unbeknown to his parents, who saw him off each morning with his Xaverian uniform on). He was a very good footballer and captained the Collyhurst Lads team, with a certain Shay Brennan playing on the wing with him, who went on to win the European Cup with Manchester United in 1968. Nobby Stiles, who was also in that '68 team and won the World Cup in '66 for England, played for Collyhurst the year Dad stopped playing too.

Dad's DNA haplogroup was R-M222, which shares an ancestral line to Niall of the Nine Hostages, a High King of Ireland in 377 CE. Their descendants were known as Ui Neill and were the most powerful monarchs of Ireland until the 11th century. Interestingly modern-day surnames which have been able to trace back their ancestry to Niall include the surname Flynn! (Flynn by name, Flynn by Nature!) Niall of the Nine Hostages got his name by taking Nine hostages, including Saint Patrick, during raids on many other

Chieftains in Ireland, England, and France…sounds like a guy not to mess with.

As previously alluded to, their marriage resulted in three children, and life happened, and this is the intro, so forgive me for missing out on 39 years of their marriage up until when Mum and Dad's working years finished, and they embarked on, what was for anyone, a rather exciting trip around the world.

They had always travelled and loved their holidays, a lot of the time with us children, mainly to Portugal and the Gower in Wales, but also to Menorca and other parts of Spain. I specifically remember a fun trip to Lanzarote too during my second year at Manchester University (with a wonderful New Year's eve dinner in a busy restaurant, and Mum, having possibly had one drink too many (i.e., 3), laughing at a man on the next table's funny nose and moustache mask, only it wasn't a mask. None of us could stop laughing for the rest of the evening). Anyway, you get the gist, lots of fun family holidays. But…when it was just them alone, they'd venture further away…to the Gambia, Israel, Cyprus, Hong Kong, etc.

This trip was going to be a much bigger adventure, though, over two months travelling for the Husband-and-wife team! The trip starts here. It's all Ray's writing, except for a few entries Melba did, or as Dad refers to her as, the cub reporter (an old journo reference to a young, often inexperienced news reporter). The words in italics are relevant (or/and irrelevant) commentary by me. I have left the words exactly as written, bar the occasional spelling, so for any grammar police, don't take it up with me! Where they mention a hotel or restaurant by name, I've looked it up and added the website details, if available, also in italics below the comment.

Please go with the flow, you'll get to understand Dad's humour; he seems to get better at writing the diary as the days go by; and, whilst, at the time, he may well have been frustrated, annoyed, and in his words 'pissed off', with some travel issues; he never stopped talking about the trip years after – particularly India, which, at the time he was less than happy with certain parts of the journey there…you'll see.

The 67 days spanned from 24th November, 1998, to 29th January 1999.

Voila!

Around The World In 67 Days

The journey really started in mid-August 1998. At least it did for Melba because she organised the whole trip, all of it, including additional clothes, visas, and all financial arrangements. Ray turned up on the day of departure, *Tuesday, 24th November 1998*

Day 1. Departed Heathrow @ .... On flight number NZ001 Air New Zealand. First stop Los Angeles, USA. Arrived at 19:00 hrs. Big surprise: upgraded to business class, Champagne all the way (see menu). *Menu obviously lost – probably by me.*

Hotel: Hollywood Roosevelt on Hollywood Boulevard- Very good. Hotel steeped in 'film' history. Oscars presented initially. Used by Clark Gable, Charlie Chaplin etc. Situated opposite Mann's Chinese theatre.

Didn't sleep well - awakened by noise from street below.

25th November

Trip from 8:15 am:

Monica Del-Ray

Venice Beach

Santa Monica

Bel Air

Beverly Hills

Sunset Boulevard

Rodeo Drive

Wilshire country club

Lunch @ Farmers Market

P.M. Universal Studios

San Fernando Valley

Melba worked as special effects on big foot.

Dinner out @ Hamlet Hamburger Restaurant - much better than name. Food excellent- quantities ridiculous, only able to eat 50% - wine good (à la Sainsburys Chardonnay)

They travelled westward. Generally, this seems to be the favoured option, and saves winding your watch forward so much! Mum arranged a round-the-world (RTW) plane ticket through a single airline alliance; it makes it easier to visit as many places as possible and pay it all in one transaction. As Dad points out, there's a lot of preparation and planning involved; it was second nature to Mum, who was the personal assistant to the Managing Director of a global consultant engineering business. Personally, I'd have loved working on a project like this 'together', but Dad clearly appreciated Mum's organisational powers!

26th November

Stay in Hollywood (near hotel) all day. Walked around until leaving for LAX @ 3:30 pm

(Managed to use mobile to contact Michael) departed for Rarotonga (Cook Isles) @ 18:50 hrs. Flight an absolute NIGHTMARE. 5 ½ hours to Honolulu - 1 ½ hours in transit followed by 6 ½ hours to Fiji, + 1 ½ hours in transit lounge, crossed date line twice…

KIA ORANA (Welcome/Long life)

…consequently, went from Thursday to Saturday and back to Friday after a further 3-hour flight from FIJI to RAROTONGA. Felt nearly dead, not 1 second's sleep since Thursday 7 am until Friday night @ 10 pm.

When we arrived at RARO, no baggage initially – turned up ½ hour later. Monsoon in progress. (Thank God for St John's Wort)

Dad would take St John's wort, a natural herbal medicine, to keep him calm. It was a strange thing for someone outwardly so confident, but you never know what can be going on inside people's heads, even close loved ones. He would swear by them and probably only took them as they were a 'Natural' source of assistance.

3

Now 4 pm *(Friday 27ᵗʰ November)*

Already been swimming - fantastic view from the hotel on beach. Hotel - Super. Tonight - BARBIE. (it's just started pouring again - locals very happy - silly billies).

Dinner: Melba had BBQ, but what a BBQ! Prawns, Fish, Beef/Pork strips. Salad nice - Superb. I went a la carte (flash git).

Seafood vol-au-vents to start + 8 massive prawns in garlic etc., with CHIPS - Magnifico. Bed by 10:00 pm. Slept very well up at 5:00 am for a cup of tea, then laid in bed until 7:00 am.

Saturday, 28ᵗʰ November

Had sun and occasional showers (I sound like Ian McCaskill). Sat on the balcony @ 7:30 am watching breakers over coral reef with a local man beach fishing with rod + line standing in sea 250 yards out, with a large plastic bucket on a string around his neck for the catch (all this seen through small binoculars which we brought with us). Another cup of coffee, and then we'll walk round for breakfast & collect the "activities for guests today" hand-out. I noted yesterday was massage, plus climbing coconut trees then, believe it or not, learn to play the Ukulele.

Had sun all day.

Pool/Sea/Pool/Drinkies/Lunch/Sea/Pool/Drinkies. 6:30 pm off to see the earth oven opened for tonight's food. Big night tonight - showtime with the local girls giving us a whirl. The evening is entitled "THE UMUKAI FEAST"- with Polynesian band, singing + dancing (unfortunately they didn't know Barefoot days!).

Great evening- food, drink, and entertainment

Ian McCaskill was a BBC weatherman in the '70s, 80's, and '90s.

Umukai Feasts – 'Umu' is the name for the Cook Islands traditional earth oven, and 'kai' is the local name for food!

As a budding Archaeologist, I'm aware of Umus – they are effectively cooking pits and a key indicator of human settlements from the past.

Sunday, 29th July

Another HOT/HOT Day.

Actually, it was only the first day, Friday, when it interspersed with monsoon-type rain.

Today we did nothing again but swim in Sea/Pool + sunbathe reading books, the odd beer/coffee, and lunch on RAROTONGA Burgers with salad + chips. Melba had steak. I had tuna, both marinated in something delicious.

It's now 5:30 pm sitting on our balcony, loving coffee and writing up the STARSHIP LOG before preparing ourselves for the evening's entertainment. (My feet are burned – underneath! - I forgot to oil them).

Rib eye steak for dinner- delicious. In bed by 10 pm.

Monday, 30th November

Circle Island Tour today.

(Just remembered an incident on Saturday night Melba covered her body with 'Head and shoulders' shampoo thinking it was After sun cream.)

Day starts very windy + cloudy; we'll see how it progresses.

7:00 am - warm/windy

Starship log 13:30hrs.

Having circled the island, we can repeat as follows

1) Captain Cook discovered the islands in 1773.

2) Main crops: Bananas/Coconuts/Taro, a type of a type of spinach normally mixed with coconut cream. /Paw Paw/Mangos/Avocado/Pineapple.

3) For medical purposes, Noni. Used in cancer treatments. (However, locals believe it only works in its natural environment mixed with other local herbs).

4) Main flowers: Hibiscus/ Frangipani, Bougainvillea

5) Spectacular trees: Poinciana (flame tree).

6) In 1350AD, catamarans left Rarotonga and landed in New Zealand 10 days later (hence the Māoris).

Now I shall finish my coffee (Melba tea) and go down for lunch. Weather still very windy with scudding clouds but warm.

N.B. Tipping is unacceptable on this island.

ACTUAL FLYING TIME TO DATE: 27 HOURS

Walk in the afternoon (2 ½ hours).

Evening's meal A La Carte (Excellent).

Saw 10 mins of New Zealand news on tv (WOW!)

Tuesday, 1st December

Melba woke up with 'red wellingtons' on à la Portugal 1997. Decided it worth seeing doctor, so took bus to capital (Avarua township). Reason for red legs (OBESITY), Melba calls it water retention. Given Diuretic tablets. (Mind you, I'm beginning to look like a Cook islander with all the food and drink and very little exercise, for me, anyway.

Spent afternoon walking along sea edge, swimming, and reading books on the beach.

17:30 hrs……… Management cocktails

1830 hrs……… Fish gourmet night.

We didn't participate in the fish gourmet didn't seem right. In fact, very few people participated. So, we had dinner with Ken Starr and his wife - no, not him silly - this couple came from Ashby de la Zouch in Leicestershire- a real gold colonial couple - very pleasant.

Obesity, ha! Mum was never overweight to any noticeable degree!

Wednesday, 2ⁿᵈ December

Bad night's sleep last night extremely windy, palm trees make a lot of noise when added to sea breaking on the reef. Woke up this morning to strong wind and cloud - still swam in sea @ 7:00 am. Last day here before travelling to Fiji. Leaving hotel at approximately 2:00 am Thursday, flight departure 4:05 am - what a stupid time, another night without sleep. People don't realise what us travellers have to put up with.

We've just established that we can sleep until 1:45 am when reception will alarm us and collect luggage for bus to airport @ 2:15am.

Weather turned out glorious by 8:30 am. hot but windy - did nothing all day except the usual:

Swim/read/lunch/drink/walk, and then dinner @ 7:00 pm for an early night's rest.

Tomorrow, we leave Rarotonga @ 4:00 am Thursday, 3ʳᵈ December, and arrive in Fiji 3 hours later on Friday, 4ᵗʰ December, mind-blowing. On walk this afternoon, we saw the incomplete Sheraton hotel, originally built using Italian (probably mafia) money, 90% complete, but Italian monies ran out. (Smells of crime, bribery, and corruption)

(This was about mid-day), a local man was asked, "when did cannibalism finish?" he replied with a huge grin, "4:30 this afternoon".

Thursday, 3rd December

Left Rarotonga @ 4:05 hrs on flight NZ45 to Fiji. Arrived at 7:00 am on Friday, 4th December.

I think the greeting is BULA! (It is).

At the airport, we received coral necklaces - I looked lovely in mine.

We're staying at the Royal Sheraton Denarau Island - very posh, very expensive e.g., everything double the cost of Rarotonga. But quality superb. (Another upgrade - room this time). Only setback is one has to be reasonably formal at all times. There's flunkies everywhere. I wouldn't be surprised if there was a botty wiper.

Weather today like a sauna! Very hot, still, and sticky. Unpacking and repacking cases to look for particular items to wear is becoming tiresome.

We've just established that they ask you to select your restaurant, garden, ocean, terrace, steakhouse, or Japanese and book before 3:30 pm.

Now 9:45 am, we've showered and changed and off to suss the place out. Tried to use the mobile for Michael and Nat but no joy.

Melba was just lying on her bed sorting out tomorrow's trip when I saw a 'gecko' scampering along the top of her counterpane; you should've seen her face!

Today we have done nothing - Melba slept on a sun bed, and I swam in the sea/pool, including out to a diving raft where I gashed my thigh and knee, but I'm a hard man, so it's ok.

Tonight, we dine in the steakhouse (all very complicated). 4:30 pm, going for a stroll now around the extensive and very, very beautiful grounds, which include a beautiful golf course that Vijay Singh (golf pro) uses when at home in Fiji.

What a funny, funny place.

Tonight, at the steak bar (everybody was there except those that had booked for a Polynesian dinner in another of the restaurants), we experienced the following:

1) Waiters/waitresses = punters.

2) Seven times we were asked if we enjoyed the starter, the main course, the wine, the water, the iced towels, or the

"ceremony" of the lighting of the kerosene lamps around the bay (approx. 300 yards long).

3) FIJI TV were filming the "ceremony," this involved two men dressed in yellow straw suit's knocking shit out of two logs whilst one young boy ran the length of the bay, lighting about 100 kerosene lamps. I said to Melba at the end, "imagine if the tv crew missed part of it and asked the boy to do it again'. Would you believe he did it TWICE more; the last time, even I could hear his wheezing from 200 yards away.

4) Four old English people were sitting at the table next to us; they ate twice the amount Melba & I could manage, plus one of their party went to the toilet and, on his return, tried to sit at our table muttering in a broad northern accent "have we had a bit of a change around here?". God, I hope I never get old.

5) Just before we went to dinner, an old Fijian biddy knocked on the door to tell us that she had come to turn the beds down. 15 mins later, she left, and all she had done was turn the bed down in a very intricate and stupid way, left us a chocolate each, and changed the towels; we only arrived 10 hours ago! Remember, some days ago, I said I was beginning to look like a "Cook islander", well, I've just seen myself in profile in a full-length mirror- for "Cook islander"

read 'A Buddha'. There's only one thing for it; I'll have to stop eating and stick to drinking!

Finally, today *Friday, 4th December,* our waitress told us, "Yes, it is always humid at this time of year, our summer," and "yes, there are lots of mosquitoes" - Wonderful!!

https://www.marriott.com/en-us/hotels/nands-sheraton-denarau-villas/overview

Point 4, Dad genuinely did not want to 'get old' to the point that he couldn't look after himself. His wish was indeed granted...he died at the end of a week he'd been playing golf and fishing.

Saturday, 5th December

After a sumptuous breakfast, we waited in the lounge for transport to our island cruise @ 9:20 am after speaking to Michael and Nat. By 9:45, the hotel stay organised a taxi for us (hold that boat). Actually, the harbour lay 2 minutes away in the taxi.

An absolutely beautiful day.

Sailed on the "Tropic See" boat to Malamala Island about 1 ½ hrs sailing, then the day was spent taking trips from the island for either snorkelling, glass bottom boat, or fishing. Terrific lunch supplied fish/steak/chicken/sausages and all the usual potatoes, nice salads, fruit, coffee, drinks, beer/wine/colas/orange, etc. were available all day free (i.e., part of the trip cost) during lunch; and travelling to and fro from the island, we were surrounded by the crew who all played guitars or ukuleles and sang beautifully. Met lots of interesting people. And the weather was blue skies & hot hot (about 33c). Getting off boat at Malamala Island, Melba fell down the steps (I'm just about to view her bruises, but she says she's ok).

Malamala Island took ten minutes to circumnavigate. Fish caught - nil, Fish seen - millions. Dinner tonight @ 8 pm in the Ocean Terrace restaurant (it's not a bad life this).

I was talking to the Fijian crew on the boat, saying it must be hell for them waking up every morning and thinking oh god! More sailing, fishing, and snorkelling again. I think they get wages as well. I was one of 2 out of 32 trippers who tried the local jungle juice 'Kava' I think it's called, made from the pepper root. It looked like the dirty washing-up water in a bowl and tasted just like it - foul. But apparently, it has some effect on the nervous system and slows it down (good for snorkelling, I was told). 9:20 pm and dinner is finished – superb meal fish cakes and chicken curry - sounds mundane? You should have seen it, e.g., the curry was served in a hollowed-out coconut with all the trimmings surrounding it. Unfortunately, because I smoke, we were placed on the periphery.

We sat bitten by mozzies', I can't feel mine, but Melba says she can feel a lump. "Sam", our man, provided a spray as soon as Melba made it obvious that she was in distress (one could tell because she screamed and leapt up onto the table!). Coffee + Brandy (Earl grey for Melba) in our a/con room before Bo Bos listening to Bula radio (English) they've just referred to Man United's bad week, losing to Tottenham in the Worthington (I can see Mike and Mark's faces from here) plus Kiddo going to Blackburn (bastard). The funny thing is they are talking about this Saturday afternoon's game with Aston Villa, and it's now 9:30 pm Saturday night here in Fiji. It looks as though I can't leave the country for 5 minutes, and Old Trafford falls to pieces.

9:45 pm, I thought the air con was playing up before I realised it was the rain absolutely pounding on the roof (big time).

Kava is effectively a 'grog', a local narcotic and sedative drink made by crushing the roots of the Yaqona plant, usually served in a communal bowl.

Man United did indeed have an 'off week' and were knocked out of the Worthington Cup, a competition I had sponsored in my capacity as Sponsorship Director for Bass

Brewers. At the end of the season, of course, United went on to win the Carling Premiership, which I also sponsored and invited Mum & dad to watch and meet Fergie and the team afterwards. They then won the FA Cup, which Dad and I went to, and finally, on 26th May 1999, won the Champions League final, which again I took Dad too, along with Mark, Natalie's husband, and some United supporting friends. The Treble was United's, never done before nor since.

Sunday, 6th December

For a change today, we're having R&R around the pool & beach. Hot hot sunshine, blue skies.

Dinner tonight is booked for the garden view restaurant. Lunch today in the steakhouse was catch of the day or a big grilled tuna steak with all the trimmings and a few glasses of New Zealand chardonnay. The hotel couldn't be bettered anywhere in the world. Every facility imaginable. Even though it's expensive by pacific standards, it's still only about the same as England (times 50% of Four Seasons), but what a difference!!

Four Seasons was a restaurant in Chobham, Surrey, the Flynn family frequented for special occasions.

Repacking tonight, but most of it done. Nice flight time tomorrow, 11:30 am, so leave here at 9ish after breakfast. And then New Zealand, here we come. Turned into humid and light rain at 4:30 pm. I suppose there's an element of luck regarding the weather in December. So, I think I've said before it is the rainy season here now (summer).

ACTUAL FLYING TIME TO DATE: 30 HOURS

What a brilliant last night in the garden view. Melba = Lobster (Fijian) Ray = Tuna

Sorbets, bits, and pieces throughout, compliments of the management, Pianist, etc., etc.- Fantastic.

We left no tip - we had no money on us - you can imagine the laughter as we legged it from the opulent ambiance with all the bowing and scraping - it's a good job we're not staying a day longer. We both think we'll have to carry our own cases to the taxi tomorrow - only 200 yds. Maids been in while we were dining, leaving us chocs and "turning down the bed"; they do everything except jump in bed with you. We will leave a few bob in the Xmas box in the lounge for them all (actually, you can't take Fijian money out of the country, so they've cracked it).

Monday 7th December

Leave Fiji on NZ32 @ 11:30 am for Auckland NZ. Weather... HOT.

Arrived in Auckland NZ @ 2:30pm but didn't arrive @ hotel until 4:30pm – Reasons: -

(i) ages to get through customs.

(ii) a ridiculous Cooks tour on a bus around Auckland before being the last to disembark at the "Rose Park Hotel" (one of the Quality chain hotels).

The Royal Sheraton, it ain't! But it's ok. Situated near the harbour in an area called Parnell. Dinner already booked for 7:30 pm. Restaurant looks very nice overlooking a large rose garden which is in bloom (Covers about 1 acre with thousands of rose trees and bushes). The fragrance is heady.

Apparently, we have to be up @ 6 am tomorrow. Breakfast @ 7 and coach pickup for our last trip at 8 am (it's all Go). First impression of Auckland not favourable. Just another city.

https://www.aucklandroseparkhotel.co.nz/

ACTUAL FLYING TIME TO DATE: 33 HOURS

Tuesday 8th December

Alarm bell 6:15 AM (we must be mad).

We've just returned back @ the hotel; it's 9:45 pm, and I'm knackered.

Day started badly - coach to Bus station, calling at other hotels. Arrived 7:45 am – sat on the bench till coach for Bay of Islands arrived. Travelled 235km to Paihia. Fortunately, driver/guide superb, clear/informative, commentating all the way. (Auckland traffic a nightmare)

Points of interest

1) Kauri trees (only 19 old ones remaining).

2) Simpson family early settlers.

3) Braeburn apples grown here.

4) All Pizza Hut Mozzarella cheese comes from N.Z.

5) Visited Waitangi treaty house and saw Māori boat-Holds 150 Warriors and 80 oarsmen - incredible.

6) Boarded Catamaran Tiger III for trips around Bay of Islands saw a large pod of Dolphins swimming alongside the boat - beautiful to see - went through hole in rock - My lunch blew away - Melba was sick most of the boat trips - landed on Motuarohia (Roberton Island) off which world's largest Marlin are caught. American author Zane Grey used to come to fish for Marlin. Weather - Sunny but windy. Sea choppy.

Long journey back. - feel it's stupid to be going on another whole day's trip to some bloody geysers tomorrow, starting at 7:20 am until 8:30 pm, but Melba is keen, so I'll have to go - I DEFINITELY DO <u>NOT</u> WANT TO GO.

The Simpson family reference is probably noted as Dad's mum had the surname 'Simpson' – My kids absolutely loved this information – that we are partly 'The Simpsons' and that any likeness of me to Homer may not be coincidental!

Wednesday 9th December

We went on the trips after all - Raymond loads of points; Melba - minus loads.

A very poor day as far as I was concerned. Roughly 500 miles (return) to see a

(i) Cave with glow worms but otherwise not a patch on the mines in Castleton (Derbyshire).

(ii) Rotorua (Fucawackawaka spelt with a w but pronounced fuc…) to see the geysers and a few Māori carvings etc, plus to be patronised by a stupid Māori woman who kept talking about "my people" and their culture whilst taking us on a golf cart train around a brick pathed road. What a load of hypocrisy (yes, I had been taken my johnnie's - St john wort).

(iii) (i and ii were interrupted by a visit to Robertons Farm) where we saw some Trout, Swans, stuffed Kiwi, and, best of all, an animal farm show while an extremely loud-mouthed girl and a normal-speaking boy put on a show with real sheep, dogs, Bull and Cow.

a) the dogs rounded up the sheep (Phil drabble must be rolling in his grave).

b) a lady from the audience sat on the Bull.

c) 2 people milked a cow.

d) 6 people fed milk from bottles to lambs.

GET A LIFE!

Got back at 8:30 pm.

Walked a mile for an evening meal but eventually found a nice French restaurant- Whole Snapper, Crepe Suzette, and coffee.

Excellent end to a CRAP Day.

(Melba thought it was great, especially the Oysters at Whakerewarewa (Rotarura)

They're funny, some people, aren't they?

(Keep meeting a man from Burton-on-Trent- he's loaded with money and tattoos. We think he may be dying - All sorts of reasons.)

(North Island - Timber and Cows)

(South Island - Sheep)

I dropped my lunch again; this time served on a moving bus.

Today Melba should have been the Cub reporter; however, your foreign correspondent (Ray) sacked her as she was useless.

Looking at the cub's notes, I see.

i) The longest man-made forest in the southern hemisphere is here in NZ (near Rotorua)

ii) Walkamo river, at 475 km, Is the longest in NZ

See what I mean?

Weather - God knows. I was on a bus all day; as you may have guessed, NZ gets a very low rating on the Ray scale.

Thursday 10th December

Wake up to RAIN. New Zealand has really blown it now. Still, it's travelling to Sydney today, so it doesn't really matter.

We leave the hotel at about 11:30 am. Flight @ 2:00 pm

Left Auckland N.Z on flight NZ105 departed at @2:15pm - flying time 3 hrs but due to time difference (2 hours behind in Oz) arrived at 3:15 pm. We still didn't arrive at our hotel, The Chateau in the Potts Point area of Sydney overlooking Elizabeth bay - 20 mins walk to Sydney Opera house, until about 5:00 pm.

ACTUAL FLYING TIME TO DATE: 36 HOURS

Hotel looks good. Unfortunately, our room on the 5th floor overlooks the street and not the sea. Weather very, very hot and sticky. Apparently, this is the first hot day they've had this summer. Dinner @ 8 pm - again, unfortunately, the terrace restaurant overlooking the bay is booked for a "do", so we're inside. Sydney, big and busy, traffic mostly.

Dinner – excellent - Market Fish catch of the day - snapper. Superb. Highlight of the meal - Ray squeezed a lemon-coloured squash all over his fish, assuming it was a lemon. Melba's comment, "I haven't got a lemon wedge".

Night view from hotel balcony fantastic - similar to films where Americans open curtains and look out over New York, etc- breath taking- I'm just about to take coffee out there and inhale the atmosphere.

Binoculars (ex-Seniors Open Golf) superb even @ night (very impressive).

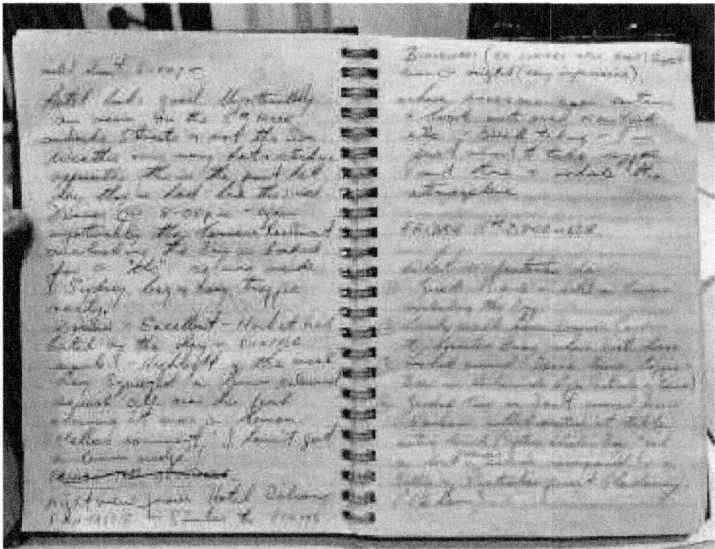

The Chateau Hotel, 14 Macleay Street, Potts Point, is no longer. It was demolished after the 2000 Sydney Olympics and is now a prestigious apartment block named Pomeroy.

Friday 11th December

What a fantastic day

1) Great F.E.B in hotel on terrace overlooking the bay.
F.E.B. – Full English Breakfast

2) Lovely walk thru botanical gardens to circular quay where boats leave.

3) Looked around opera house, coffee and beer in harbourside cafe (outside, of course).

4) Guided tour on boat around Sydney harbour whilst seated at a table eating lunch (options, chicken, beef, fish, a host of various salads accompanied by a bottle of Australia's finest chardonnay (1 ½ hours).

5) In the afternoon, we boarded a coach for a very informative tour of Sydney, stopping at a few interesting spots, including Bondi beach, DOYLES restaurant @ Watson Bay, Gap Park (entry to Sydney harbour), and Mrs Macquarie's chair.

Whilst on Luncheon boat, saw a yacht with its own helicopter on board (lands and takes off from the yacht. We also saw Kookaburra I AND II -Australia's American cup challenge boats.

BONDI = Aborigine for "where the waves meet the sand".

Therefore, all beaches should be Bondis.

Agapanthus - Similar to Flax flower

Callistemon - Bottle Brush tree

Paddington area - most houses have extremely ornate Ironwork in front. This dates back to the early settlers whose boats used pig iron as ballast. Once they arrive in Oz at a bay near Paddington - they dumped the pig iron in the bay hence all the framework around old houses in Paddington (referred to as lace) Double bay - incredibly expensive land for a house 4 million dollars.

Recently a house was bought on double bay point for 20 million dollars and then demolished so the new owner could build one to his liking.

Back @ hotel by 5:30 pm.

Dinner tonight will be in a lovely Thai restaurant we've seen 2 minutes from our hotel.

Dinner was superb - Crab cakes, prawns, and duck- (far too much) but delicious - Wine divine.

Tried to book @ Doyles for tomorrow (in water taxi there and back-but they book 50%, and one takes one's chance on the remaining 50% - not worth the travel, so will go elsewhere.

Tomorrow we'll spend the day on Manly beach. Walk through Botanical gardens again to "Circular Quay", do a bit of shopping, and then get a 30 min ferry to Manly beach - sounds good to me.

Coffee on my terrace overlooking Sydney city, and then we're off to bed.

https://www.doyles.com.au

Saturday 12th December

Another incredible day - Weather - Blue skies and 34c Sun.

Breakfast on terrace, walk thru botanical garden and circular quay. Thirty minutes ferry and Manley beach. Incredible surf and play in. Lunch a bit iffy - butty and orange juice (Melba loved it), followed by a beer in Harry's sports bar. I think it was a bookies because of all the TVs around the walls (Melba wasn't too keen). Ferry to the quay. Bit of shopping underneath the opera house. Walk back thru park, and bingo, here we are on hotel balcony (ours), ready to prepare for the night out.

Of all the places I've ever been to, Sydney is the best, taking everything into account.

i)   Weather

ii) Scenery

iii) Culture

iv) People (confusing, isn't it?)

v)   Affluence

vi) Cost of living

vii) The food

Sydney has been a real eye-opener for Melba and me.

Names of interest

1) Magnolia Grandiflora

2) Jacaranda (Bluebell tree)

Just a thought before we go out to dinner. I don't know about flying around the world, I think we've eaten around the world, and we've got the figures to show it. Rather portly.

After great deliberation, I've decided that the 'Cub' can have one more attempt at the 'Log' - she's not very happy about it, but I've primed her with all the necessary information so here goes.

Our last night in Sydney

Byline Melba Flynn

A very enjoyable meal, we started with a dish of appetizers which included oysters with a very tasty dressing, smoked salmon, artichoke pie, sun-dried tomato with cheese on toasted bread, and small fried squid - that was just for starters! The main meal was Snapper on a bed of steamed vegetables in a delicious sauce. We finished off with Pecan Tarte Tatin (one portion between us).

The owner (French) was extremely nice and interesting, and a Singaporean waiter who very kindly gave us a list of places to visit when we arrive in Singapore. Very good evening!

(No wonder Melba's still a cub reporter).

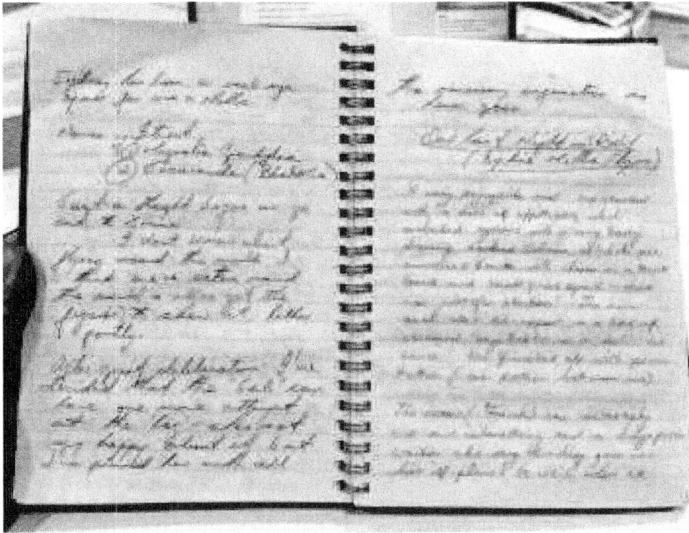

Sunday 13th December

Back on our travels today, a biggy! We're off to Brisbane (1 ¼ hours flight), which is 1 hour behind Sydney, so we'll arrive at the same time as we take off.

ACTUAL FLYING TIME TO DATE 37 ¼ HOURS

Left Sydney on flight AN128 @ 13:55 hours and arrive in Brisbane at 14:10 hours (local time).

Met by Ness, Michael, Luke, and Holly. Marvellous to see them all again. Weather - overcast and warm. Arrived at their house in Mooloolah 40 minutes later after stopping at a fruit farm shop - the array of fruits was incredible, and the prices so cheap. The house is lovely, in a beautiful setting.

The evening consisted of champagne, prawns, smoked Tuna (done by Michael in a kipper burner), raw tuna, homemade bread and salad, and fresh fruits. The kids played in the pool for hours (they're both very good swimmers).

At 9:00 pm, we returned to our house in the garden (the kids' playroom) with all mod-cons. Tea and coffee making, TV, Books, Settee. Slept fitfully (very warm).

Now... this Michael is not me, but Vanessa's husband (Michael numero 2). Luke & Holly are her children from her marriage to Huw Daniels, who passed away a few years earlier when the children were both very young. Since this trip, Vanessa & Michael have Lily too (named after Dad's Mum).

Monday 14ᵗʰ December

Awake at 5:45 am, joined by Holly @ 6:15, Luke @ 6:45. Michael off to work (pinstriped suit, white shirt, and very tasteful tie, black brogue shoes?).

Swam in the pool at about 7:00 am, breakfast around pool - fresh fruit, coffee, and bread baked during the night. Weather cloudy, warm with a hint of rain. Reading paper delivered at 5 am. United draw with Spurs. Short walk around Ness and Mike's house. Impression - walking around Wentworth estate but with wider roads (no footpath), houses dotted around approx. one acre each, and the whole scene surrounded on one side by heavily wooded hills and lowland opposite. Both kids swim and dive like dolphins.

Ribeye Steak dinner.

Tuesday 15ᵗʰ December

7:30 am- Golf @ Caloundra G.C. with Michael and his friend Russell. 1 Birdie 1 par in 9 holes.

(Forget the other 9) Very small-headed clubs and trainers.

Michael's taken a day off work.

Afternoon - visit to Steve Irwin's Queensland. Reptile and fauna park alligators, crocodiles, snakes, and 168-year-old Henrietta tortoise originally captured by Charles Darwin and sent to England for research - brilliant place. See photo of Ray and Holly with a python!

Evening BBQ around pool - BoBo's @ 9 pm (Keith Pinner phoned at 9:30 pm)

Tried to contact Nat and Mark several times, but no luck.

https://www.australiazoo.com.au/

Wednesday 16th Dec

Tried Nat and Mark again no luck, left a message.

Kids off to party at 10 am

Melba and Ness - Shopping, I stayed around pool, swimming, reading, cleaning lady here for 2 hours (I really don't believe it). Michael at work. A very lazy day for me.

Snapper and chips for dinner (superb fish) sat on the balcony chatting until 9-30.

Thursday, 17th December

7:45 am here - 9:45 pm England tried Nat and Mark, no reply, left a message. By 9 am, we were all sitting on Kings Beach (Michael, unfortunately working). Then about 11:00, we moved to Shelly beach, ½ a mile away. We lunched @ Moffatt beach, Mexican burger (mmm mmm mmm). It's still only 3:00 pm, and we're back at the house in the pool - it feels like 6:00 pm.

I've never experienced a sun as hot as this. At the beach, it was absolutely burning, and I was heavily oiled (30+). I would not be surprised if my feet blistered underneath. Talk about walking on hot coals. That must be child's play after the beach. Lovely dinner (Chicken fish) originally looked like raw pink tuna, but when cooked looks and tastes like chicken. Melba's pre-dinner drink - a pint of Cinzano (I kid you not) she sang all night. Rained at 8:15 pm in bed by 9:05 pm. (storm in Brisbane - golf ball hail - Cars badly damaged).

Friday, 18th December

Up @6:00 am

Temperature @ 9 am – 37c in shade. I have never experienced a sun as hot as this.

Spent the day around the pool reading and swimming (Bill Bryson - Notes from a Small Island - brilliantly funny and relatable too).

This evening we're off out to dinner somewhere with Michael, Ness, Russell (ex-golf), and his wife (Juliet). Still can't contact Nat and Mark. Saw a Possum on the fig tree in garden.

Holly seemed to change dresses at least five times a day. At 3:30 pm, we had one almighty storm (real tropical), lightning, thunder, and rain, but no hail. Mark phoned - all well, phone was out of order. Lovely evening meal out at the Tivoli. Bed at midnight. My God!

Saturday, 19th December

Up @ 6 am – Swim in the pool, then off fishing to Pumicestone passage. Only small Sea Bream and Whiting caught. Very small. Lunch around the pool and back to Steve Irwin's reptile park specifically to see the daily feeding of the crocodiles. I'm booked to wrestle Charlie @ 1:30 pm - complete sell out – result - I beat him with two falls and a submission. This evening we're off to some friends at Shelley beach for cheese and wine. Weather brilliant until 3:15, then another big storm. Jorge (German) and Julies' house for wine and cheese - v.nice people. Absolutely knackered by 9:15 pm and so to bed.

Sunday, 20ᵗʰ December

Surprise, surprise, a cloudy start to the day. Temperature 26c wind - Time 7:00 am.

7:46 am - 29c Hot sun and blue skies.

From 11:30 until 6:30, we spent the day @ Chris & Natalie's house @ Kawana Waters on the river near the sea. Imagine a Villa (bigger and higher than any in Portugal) fronting onto the river with the large boat mooring in front (carpeted!). On the jetty are two recesses to hold fishing rods, and underneath each of them, a water holding tank for either bait or the catch. Glen has a wholesale Fish business, Lobsters, crabs, fish, etc. The house probably costs £1 ½ million. You can imagine the food and wine (on a revolving centre table) seating 12 people, absolutely 'out of this world' and very pleasant people. Bed @8:30pm. Slept very badly - fan noisy, very humid night.

Monday, 21ˢᵗ December

Alarm went off at 5:15 am, playing golf @ 6:30 am. Caloundra golf course with Michael and Russell. Back home by 9 am, and Michael straight to work. Vanessa and Luke, and Holly partying today. One party 9:30 am start and the second one about 2 pm. so Melba and I have the place to ourselves all day - Reading, Swimming (book is Bill Bryson's notes from a small island - brilliant).

Weather 35c sun and 70% humidity (very sweaty).

Apparently, in parts of the Brisbane area, the humidity was 96%.

Terrific evening, dinner at home on the deck. Robin (anaesthetist from Melbourne ex Frimley hospital last 17 years) and his wife Karen (nurse ex Great Ormond Street) and their four children (1 Turner disease and 1 epileptic). Super family.

Robin trying to arrange golf for Michael and me at his golf club.

Bed @ 1:50 am and - oh my god - we're travelling to Noosa tomorrow (Melba and I) for a 3-day holiday (present from Ness and Michael).

A stick insect 10"long with wings like a bird landed on Michael's head. He thought it was great.

Tuesday 22nd December

Up @ 6:45 am - lovely fresh, sunny day 7 am (28c)

Leaving shortly for Noosa. Last night we were told that this place is the Cannes and St Tropez of Australia. Looking forward to it.

12:30 pm well, here we are at Noosa heads, staying at the Tingirana Noosa Hotel. I've just walked through the (opened) French window, and I'm on the lawn 10 yards from the beach with the surf crashing in. The room has all mod cons. View from bed (don't be naughty) is sensational. In front of hotel is courtyard and covered exit/entrance to main road shopping area about 200 yards long. Parks at both ends. Nessa and Luke drove us here about 50 minutes from their home, so this is us until Thursday (Christmas Eve), when Michael, Ness, and the kids will join us for lunch (pre-booked) at a fantastic-looking restaurant 100 yards from here on the beachfront. Serving seafood predominantly.

Ness and Luke have left now after a quick dip in the ocean, so were going to explore then have some lunch. We've decided that restaurant food here in Australia Is the best we've ever had anywhere.

For tonight's dinner, we dined at Grenny's. Our cub reporter has begrudgingly agreed to describe the food:

Raymond's meal consisted of sautéed kidneys on puff pastry cases, followed by fresh seafood in filo pastry accompanied by various vegetables (two of which I didn't know). Melba's meal was green salad with tomatoes and, after, a rack of Lamb and various vegetables. It was declared that both meals were delicious. Dark coffee and cappuccino were taken with a nutty chocolate fudge to finish off with. It must also be noted that Raymond went out with his trousers half-mast!

It was declared she'll have to be sacked again.

https://tingirana.com.au

Wednesday, 23rd December

Awake @ 5:45 am after a good night's sleep (were both knackered yesterday), swam in the sea at 7 am now were off to Eduardo's restaurant for a FEB with Australian additions, e.g., Fruit and Damper bread. The breakfast selection was incredible - pancakes, Fish, etc. Spent the day on beach in sea-blue skies and hot sun (30c). The only downer today was reading the international Daily Mail - Lynda Lee-Potter et al. in which I read of Man United's demise. Went without lunch today after all we've eaten; it's the least we can do (people will begin to think we're Welsh).

Tonight, we ate at a Chinois/Thai restaurant. Spring rolls, crab cakes, seafood curry (green), and king prawns with cashew nuts, etc. for Melba + lovely two bottles of wine. Superb meal $110 = £42.

Bed at 9:45 pm.

Re: 'Welsh' comment - Mum & Dad had a place on the Gower, Wales, where they would often joke about how many locals frequenting the local fish & chip shop on the beach were rather overweight.

Eduardo's by the River closed permanently during Covid lockdowns.

Thursday, 24th December (Christmas Eve)

Hard to imagine. No carols, no Father Christmas - Bliss. I've had to wait 62 years for this – if I died now - aah!

Up @ 6:30 am, Swim in the sea shopped for muffins, butter jam, and orange juice. Breakfast on the balcony. We couldn't face Eduardo's breakfast. After all, we've scheduled a big lunch with Ness, Michael, and the kids at 1 pm. Weather blue sky, hot sun, and a very welcome breeze.

Super meal, after which we swam in the sea (Melba and Ness went shopping) until we left for home about 5 pm. Carols around the tree (7' 6" tall) bed at 9:30 pm - Big day tomorrow.

Dad was not a big fan of Christmas.

Friday, 25th December (Christmas Day)

Up at 6 am (sore throat and headache). Merry Christmas, kids, didn't bother us, although they had been up since 3 am. After tea and the opening of presents each from under the tree, we all drove to the beach: 'Kings in the surf' for a swim and then back to the house for hot croissants, coffee, and Bucks fuzz at 10:30 am.

Weather blue skies and hot hot sun. 10:30 until 12:30 opening pressies followed by swimming, reading, etc.

2 pm oysters, bugs (like small lobsters), prawns, etc., around the pool. Wine(s) marked out of ten – nothing's under 8. This all lasted until 5 pm.

At 7:30 pm, we sat down to the turkey, etc., etc. Re., the Bugs, imagine eating four whole lobsters each person; that is what we consumed together with 1 slice of ciabatta bread (lovely spelling). The prawns (I had 10) were approximately 10 inches long. It's now 5:15 pm, and most of the party have reached that siesta stage. I'm still going strong, and the throat and head appear to have cured themselves. Could be down to the St John's wort which I've circulated.

Visited the Clampits up the hill - Sat around their bonfire smoking a peace pipe and shooting tinnies off the woman's head whilst she smoked her clay pipe (only joking).

Came down to a superb traditional Turkey dinner with hats, crackers, and presents.

Afterwards, I said to Michael, "I suppose it's only fools and horse - but 1995 version"- he replied, "we call it only fools and foals" - Superb evening. Spoke to Nat, Jack and Michael and Kat… and Mark not talking to me (nor Joe, Charlie, or Gemma) bed at about 10 pm.

The Bugs referred to are Moreton Bay bugs, and dad came back raving about them. They are named after Moreton Bay in Brisbane and are a type of small slipper lobster, rare over here in Europe. I tried them for the first time last year in Sydney and now know how good they are…Dad was spot on.

Saturday, 26th December

Awake @ 6 am, blue sky, hot sun. After a swim, we breakfasted, including about 30 of the 10" prawns. At lunchtime, Robin, Karen, and their four children arrived. The day was spent eating oysters, bugs, prawns, and smoked Salmon with wine all day.

Sunday, 27ᵗʰ December

Up at 5:15 am to play 18 holes of golf at Twin Waters G.C. with Michael and Robin – Superb course; used buggies, so didn't feel heat as much. Afterwards to Robin's house @ Buderim for lunch and swim back at Ness's house at 3:30 pm, temperature 38c, humidity 38%. So, I'll finish now. Drink my coffee and get in that pool. A very hot evening at 8 pm temperature still 31c humidity 75%. Had a go on Ness' ride on mower (with headlights); see photos. *(Unfortunately, I can't find these photos)*

Evening meal of home-smoked calamari, fried veg, and salad.

https://www.twinwatersgolfclub.com.au

Bed at 9 pm.

Monday, 28th December

Awake at 6:30 am. Saw 'TAHLIA', the Butcherbird which occasionally calls. It was just sitting on the deck rail, obviously waiting to be fed.

10:00 am, we're all off to Bribie Island with the boat for a day's fishing/picnic - temperature 35c - blue skies - memories of Rogers boat are 'flooding' my mind.

Great day, launching boat was a piece of cake. Special launching areas into river-like water it's actually called Pumicestone passage; it was also made easier because Michael was captain and Vanessa was first mate, Melba, the kids, and I were passengers. We motored over to the island and fished for a few hours, walking in foot-deep mud, surrounded by soldier crabs. No fish.

We then picnicked, followed by a walk through a jungle for 1 ½ miles in steaming heat until we came to the South Pacific Sea. The beach was about 5 miles long with white powdery sand and crashing rollers. Then it was the walk back through the jungle (Melba mozzied twice), another 1 ½ hours fishing (no fish), and then back onto the boat and home about 6:00 pm.

Dinner in, and bed, very tired. Oh! I forgot about the Pelicans, hundreds of them flying around and sitting on top of main water channel markers.

Butcher birds are songbirds closely related to the Australian magpie. They are named as such from the way they 'Butcher' their prey – including lizards, which they impale on a thorn or a 'crack' in a tree.

Tuesday 29th December

Didn't wake until 7:30 this morning, heavy night last night. Weather cloudy this morning, but still 29c sun 65% humidity. After breakfast, it's the 'tip' run with all the accumulated bottles, etc., approx. two lorry loads. Melba and Vanessa are off shopping. Mid-day, we're off to Underwater World. On way to offload bottles, saw 'The Wallabies' (Australia Rugby team) home training ground at Caloundra. Collected some beer, wine, and a pie each for Michael and myself. The pies here are a big item and are delicious. At the restaurant tonight, it's BYO (bring your own drinks). We also ordered a 'get you and your car home' (called a go-drive). Somebody drives your car home for you with you in it and is followed by another vehicle to take your driver back to base. The visit to Underwater World was brilliant, sharks, the lot. Whilst there, we saw and held the 'Blue' starfish. This confirmed that the blue starfish we picked up in the Rarotonga was not plastic after all, as we had assumed.

Note from yesterday in the forest: Melba and Luke walking together when Luke said he wanted to go to the toilet. Melba asked if it was for a wee. Luke said "No, the other."

So Melba said, "It's okay, Luke, I've got some toilet paper."

To which Luke replied, "it's alright, grandma, it was only a fart."

Dinner tonight was at The Boat Shed at Maroochydore. The kids slept over at Robins and Karen's.

Super meal, Caesar salad with battered anchovies, eggs, and cheese starters, charcoaled Tuna, potatoes, and veg. Melba - spring rolls and lamb fillets in rosemary and honey with garlic mashed potatoes. Bed at 11:45 pm, after talking to Nat and Jack (Charlie & Gemma's birthday).

https://www.visitsealife.com/sunshine-coast

I recently ate at The Boat Shed when I was over in Australia on a business trip. I flew up to the Sunshine Coast to stay with Vanessa, Michael & Luke for a wonderful few days. This restaurant is very relaxed, we sat outside by the water, and the food was wonderful – especially the scallops and the prawns! It's also the perfect place for my favourite Margarita sundowners (pictured).

https://www.theboatshed.com.au

Wednesday, 30th December

Up at 8:30 am - very tired weather, slightly cooler, 28c with passing cloud. Pool has been replenished with salt, chlorine, etc., and looks very exciting. We all decided last night that instead of going to a campsite and swimming in an icy lagoon and staying until late at night around a campfire BBQing ribeye steaks (no doubt surrounded by mozzies), we would do nothing.

Certainly, suit's me fine the way I feel. I've also got a good book to finish, "Shoot to kill" by Michael Asher. His life from the day he joined the Paras at Aldershot in 1972 - a great read.

Dinner at home. I went to bed at 8:30 pm.

Thursday, 31st December (New Year's Eve)

Wake up at 8:15 am (nearly 12 hours sleep) to rain, all over grey skies. 2 pm - Rain has finally stopped. I'm tired, and I've got a cold sore. It's beginning to get very clammy. Most of today is preparing for tonight's dinner, eight adults and seven children. Terrific New Year's Eve. Great meal, wine, and company. The only sour note was that Robin (the anaesthetist) got called out, first about 9 pm, to a patient who had suddenly become ill. He returned about 11 pm and got called out an hour later to the same patient. When he returned about 1:30, he told us the man had died and that he'd had to tell his wife over the phone. Who would be a doctor?

Melba and I managed to keep going until 3:30 am New Year's Day, leaving Ness, Michael, and Russell, who went to bed about ½ hour later.

Friday 1st January 1999

Awake at 7:15 am, somehow, I made porridge for three kids, only slightly burning the pan. Not feeling too clever. Just spoke to Mark back in England.

Weather pouring rain - looks as though it's set for the day.

Got to pack shortly; we're off again tomorrow for three days in Brisbane, it's all go. It's 2 pm New Year's Day, and I'm back in bed watching TV with Melba. It's still raining hard, but the temperature is 25 degrees.

Fell asleep until 5 pm, showered, dinner at 6:30 pm, 1 beer, and bed at 8 pm - Happy New Year.

Saturday, 2nd January 1999

Woke at 6 am poor night's sleep - weather constant rain, which we're told will last until Monday. Still, we've had our fair share of sunshine, and at least it's warm. Trip to Brisbane cancelled - rain stopped play - we shall probably rearrange for Wednesday and Thursday after Luke's Thursday birthday party @ the Rollerdome.

Even though it's pouring, we're off to Kenilworth, leaving at 11:30. You'll love this next bit... we travelled to Kenilworth in monsoon-type rain for about an hour. We debussed at Booloumba creek, where we started our trek through a rainforest still in monsoon rain. At a point where we had to cross a river, Michael shouted out, "Quick, I've got a leech on my leg; let me have your lighter, Ray" he then burnt off the leech. He was quickly followed by Vanessa. By the time we'd arrived at the gold mine (extinct) entrance 3km away, we were all very aware of the leeches, which literally jump on one from below and from above. When we returned to the car, Luke was the latest victim; we removed it with one of my lighted cigarettes. Just as I was feeling pretty lucky, I saw one entering my trainer, so I quickly burnt it off. The total score was Michael 2, Vanessa 3, Luke 1, Ray 1, Melba 0, Holly 0.

As soon as we got home, I went for a shower to find that the leech in my shoe had already penetrated the skin through my sock, and even as I write ½ hour later, it is still bleeding. Melba's big worry is that it is still around somewhere in our room.

The blood eventually stemmed, and we had a super meal of fillet steak, olive oil potatoes, and salad with some lovely red Nottage wine. We followed the meal with a board game similar to Trivial pursuits (travelling around Great Britain), which I was lucky to win, and Melba was unlucky to be last! (p.s. Holly had 1 leech, after all, in her trousers).

In bed at 11 pm

Sunday, 3rd January 1999

Up at 9:30 am - change of plan. We're off to Brisbane today, catching the 12:17 pm train from Landsborough. We shall return with Michael tomorrow via Mount Coot-Tha.

Changed trains at Caboolture on way, passing very, very close to Glass House Mountains. Train stopped at roughly 30 stations arriving in Brisbane (Roma St) at 2:15 pm. Taxi to Marriott hotel 23rd floor overlooking river and city - beautiful room and view. Went for a walk along river for lunch at 'Fridays' after a brief walk around the city centre, taking in the famous casino (from outside) situated inside the treasury building, a superb piece of architecture; we retired to our hotel room for a rest! Tonight, we're booked into a seafood restaurant called Pier Nine for 8 pm, weather brightening up. I've got the impression that the "Cub" has forgotten that she has agreed to describe the evening meal, which was the best I have ever experienced - at Pier Nine. The meal was as follows - over to the "Cub".

Starters – Ray = 6 lots of oysters in a kinda bloody Mary tots x 6. Melba had…

The CUB speaks but not until Monday 4ᵗʰ Jan 99…

Ray - "best meal he ever had or will have". Unbeatable.

Dad's writing above has most definitely been influenced by the odd glass of wine and possibly the "Blood Mary' Oyster shots too…

I didn't know I'd written last night's meal because the 'Cub' has agreed to describe the meal in detail; before I pass the log over to her, I must admit to a raging hangover...

The Cub speaks:

Raymond's meal started with 6 Cajun oyster shots followed by chargrilled swordfish accompanied by hot Thai beef salad and, of course, chips. Melba had noodles with crab (sand) and shrimp, and different vegetables with a side dish of Asian wok-fried greens. Very enjoyable! What a difference in styles!

https://www.marriott.co.uk/hotels/travel/bnedt-brisbane-marriott-hotel

Pier Nine is also no longer – it's closed to make way for a $ 2.1 billion waterfront precinct – in construction at the time of writing.

Monday 4ᵗʰ January 99

Awake at 8 am feeling like death. Weather - pouring rain, and we're supposed to be going on a paddle boat up the river.

We eventually booked out of the hotel at 10:15 pm – rain stopped. Breakfast at the "Muffin break". Bagels with egg, bacon and cheese, coffee, and a pint of pure, freshly squeezed orange juice cost £3. Incredible, and it was superb.

Walked around botanical gardens and along the riverbank until 12:30 pm, when we went on our paddle boat ride (like a Mississippi paddle boat). Unfortunately, there were lots of young Japanese girls who never stopped talking and giggling, making it impossible to hear what the guide was telling us. Brisbane has some fantastic modern high-rise architecture. Everything is clean and bright. Michael picked us up at 4:30 pm and took us to Mount Coot-Tha - where the view over Brisbane was breathtaking, back at Vanessa's about 7:30 pm to some delicious thick homemade soup. Red wine and coffee. We finished the evening playing Trivial Pursuits which was won by Michael. Melba was unlucky again and came last. Bed at 11 pm.

Tuesday, 5ᵗʰ January (Luke's birthday)

Woke up at 7 am - Weather hot sun, rain, hot sun, rain, and getting worse. We're all going to the Rollerdome for Luke's birthday party. I can feel a headache coming on. I'd better double up on the St John's wort. Rollerdome party from 10:00 am to 12:00 pm. Everybody had a great time. Melba even skated. I got quite bored and went for several walks and smokes. Saw Julie and Jorge and Karen again. Maybe for the last time. Very nice people. Sun has come out at last, very hot, but there's always the danger of a cloud burst as I look around. Melba and Ness have gone shopping again, leaving Michael, the kids, and I to our own devices. The afternoon turned out very pleasant, so it was swimming pool, deck chair, reading, and sunbathing.

For Luke's adults' party tonight, it's leg of lamb, etc., super evening meal. Nice to speak to Nat and Jack. Luke dressed up, so we all had to do likewise, including ties. Bed at 9 pm.

https://www.rollerdrome.com.au

Wednesday, 6ᵗʰ January 1999

Awake at 6:30 am - Swim in the pool, shower, shave - Hot sun. At approx. 8:30 am Michael started his day by falling out of a cupboard some 10" high; fortunately, he only suffered superficial cuts and bruises and a probable broken toe. I've given him a note excusing boats and performing light duties only. It's now 9 am, and the bloody clouds have appeared again. Fortunately, the sun reappeared, and we all enjoyed a lovely day in 28 degrees sun and blue skies. Pool, books, and drinks. Evening meal in. Cajun chicken. Weather like the best possible day in England. Melba's into pints of Red Cinzano now. She's finished all the white. We finished the evening playing Trivs. Michael was lucky to win, and I was unlucky to come last (1 piece of pie) bed at 11 pm.

Thursday, 7th January (Bin Day)

Up at 7 am - deaf as a door post. Sun and cloud. 10-30 am off to the beach with the surfboard. (Happy Valley Beach). I was useless on the surfboard, couldn't even get it out to sea, let alone stand up on it. Luke and Holly were excellent on the board. Melba paddled beautifully.

P.M. Michael shopping for tonight's homemade fish curry. Raymond shopping for gin and cigs. Weather warm but overcast. The rest of the afternoon was spent reading in the garden. Another Bill Bryson book entitled 'Neither here nor there', can highly recommend it. Michael has been busy most of the afternoon preparing tonight's dinner. The menu is as follows – Poppadums with a traditional assortment of pickles. Tandoori king prawn (10" long) on a bed of crisp lettuce, Swordfish with mushrooms in a mild coconut and lime korma sauce. Succulent baby green beans spiced with chilli and garlic. Fried spinach and potatoes in a mustard seed curry. Chilli, garlic, and coriander naan bread, I can hardly wait. We are eating at 7:30 pm. Unfortunately, at the time of writing, it's only 5:30 pm - 2 hours to wait. At 6:30pm, we had Margaritas and the Poppadom, etc. Only 1 hour to go. The smells from the kitchen are mmm mmm

mmm! I'm having a gentle G +T to while the time away, sitting in a rocking chair on the deck (veranda) listening to the Cicadas (big crickets) and watching the occasional Kangaroo bound by or the Parrots, Sea eagle, or Cockatoos strut their stuff.

It seems somewhat over the top to give 10/10 superb to one meal consisting of so many dishes, but that's my marking for a terrific meal. We're ending the evening on the deck with "Extracts from a journey around the world". Actually, the evening ended with another boring game of TRIVS. At least it is when you're playing against Michael (clever dick). I refused to play; it's bad for my psyche. They all called me a miserable sod, but I didn't care, so there! Bed at 11 pm.

Friday, 8ᵗʰ January

Up at 7:30. Ears still playing up. Can you imagine the conversations Melba and I are having "yes, you've got beautiful eyes too."

Today we're off to Harry's Hut for a BBQ in a rainforest. 1 ½ hours inland for Mooloolah. Apparently, the thing to watch out for here is not leeches so much as snapping Turtles in the creek we shall be swimming and fishing in. I'm told it's Red in colour, caused by the tea tree oil trees surrounding the lake - can't wait. After a 1hr 40min drive the last 30 minutes over an unmade road with potholes 2- 3 ft deep, we arrived at Harrys Hut. The Hut is a rusted corrugated shack on the Noosa River, surrounded by camping areas with barbeques and jetties for boats to tie up. It has to be borne in mind that this is all in the back of beyond. The forestry workers do an incredible job in creating and maintaining the areas.

The Chicken carcass brought along to bait the traps for prawns and small fish bait quickly attracted the Iguanas (lizards about 4'0" long with blue flicking tongues and about as thick as a lamp post). It really is a lovely spot, and the river, about as wide as the Thames at Windsor (and 90ft deep in parts), really is red and like swimming in Tea. (See pictures, hopefully). One's skin feels fantastic when one gets out.

We fished most of the time. Michael had 1 bite, which completely took his live prawn, and caught a Tarpon (about 1 pound) on a small rainbow fish; I didn't have a bite. But it was a lovely day enjoyed in hot sunshine. On the way back, we came upon four wallabies. Trampolining about, lovely sight. Tonight, we're eating out at Harry's restaurant, no relation to Hut or Ramsdens. We shall also be engaging a go-driver which I believe I've described earlier on. Excellent meal, even if a little bit too much and creamy. Sampled

South African beef skewered in a thick yellow sauce made of God knows what. Main course Duckling on bed of mash with various vegetables built in. Sweet, chilled Zabaglione, expresso coffee. Went to bed at 11:15 pm feeling disgustingly full.

https://parks.des.qld.gov.au/parks/cooloola/camping

https://www.harrysonbuderim.com.au

Saturday, 9th January

Wake at 7:30 am feeling like death. Rib aching, both ears blocked, and very sore.

I've just learned that Vanessa was sick during the night; not too surprised because even I felt a bit icky. Michael has very kindly been to town to purchase some Earex for me; all I need now is a rib cage splint. Eee, I am having a reet good time.

9:30 am shaved, showered, drops applied. Breakfasted on fruit juice, croissants, and coffee, I now feel human. Weather sunshine 33c, humidity 65%. Decisions ongoing as to how we will spend our last day here. We travel early tomorrow to Cairns. I find it difficult to believe how all that time has flown by. It only seems yesterday that we set eyes on Vanessa, Michael, Luke, and holly at Brisbane airport.

Why throughout have I written % for degrees?

I obviously changed them all – every temperature note has been a number and the percentage sign (XX%) – wonder if Ness pointed it out?

The hospitality shown to Melba and me by Vanessa and Michael has been fantastic, especially as it's been over such an extended period. They have gone out of their way every day not only to make us feel welcome and comfortable but also to organise for us and enjoy all the wonderful nights around, some of which have involved a lot of driving for them. We've certainly appreciated every moment we've spent here, and to think I didn't want to come initially. Stupid boy!

After a lazy morning, everybody felt tired after last night. We went to Kings beach for a swim in the sea, that is everybody except Melba and me. I couldn't go in because of my ears. After the beach, we retired to the boardwalk restaurant overlooking the harbour for coffee, beer, and sandwiches.

All consumed to the strains of a 4-piece combo band singing such songs as "On the wild side" super day.

In Vanessa's writing: 'Grandad now telling tales of the war to Luke and Holly! (8:24 pm) - remember the barbed wire (also telling tales! Horse bit his arm off!).

Last evening's meal, delicious. Rib eye fillet steak, potatoes in olive oil, broccoli, and French beans accompanied by a cheeky little chardonnay. BO BOS at 10 pm.

I presume the song was Lou Reed's "Walk on the Wild Side".

Sunday, 10th January 1999 (Departure Day - Not nice)

Awake at 6:30 am flight 9:45 am no. AN62 to Cairns. Michael, Ness, Luke, and Holly took us to the Airport. Not nice saying goodbye to them all. They waited another 30 mins after we boarded the plane, as we could see them in the departure lounge at the window. Arrived in cairns at 11:45 pm met by a young dutchman ex-marine now married to an Australian who took us to the Parm Royale Hotel. 15 mins from the airport. Superb hotel and room. There are three decent size pools, 1 for diving 4 metres deep. All towels provided even for day trips and the barrier reef, for example. Weather hot, hot sun 37c and not as humid as I expected. Today will be a relaxing day we're both shattered (bad night's sleep last night).

https://palmroyale.com.au

ACTUAL FLYING TIME TO DATE 39 ¼ HOURS

Insufficient beds around all three pools. I think the Germans are here because 2 or 3 pairs of bed have towels and books but no people for the past hour (Towels and books may go swimming if they don't turn up shortly).

We've decided to take the hotel bus into Cairns at 4 pm. It only takes 15 minutes and return on the 7:15 bus, having eaten in between. We have to be ready for our pickup at 7 am tomorrow for our boat trip to the Barrier reef. Tea/dinner on the Boardwalk in Cairns overlooking the harbour, full of million £ boats. Fantastic meal but stupidly large portions, e.g., Melba's prawn salad = 10 number 10" prawns as thick as my leg. Together with Sainsbury's delicacy of salad together with a loaf and ½ pound of butter. Mine was Barramundi grilled fish, same salad, and 1 cart of chips ridiculous. Price incl. Wine, water, and coffees = $50 = £20.

Bed at 9 pm to the sound of heavy rain - well, it is rainy season.

Monday, 11th January

Awake at 5-45am. Trip to Barrier reef - coach to Cairns Harbour. Catamaran to port Douglas 1 ½ hrs, change to the Wavedancer catamaran- sail for another 1 hour to Low Iles, where we snorkelled. Trip in glass bottom boat, lay on beach, lunch on board. Weather superb, Sun 35c light breeze on way back one of the crew sang and played guitar

63

brilliantly, back at hotel 7:15 pm. Dinner in the Colossus restaurant at 8 pm. There had to be one didn't there, and we found it. A crap restaurant, and after all we've said about the food in Australia. I shan't give it the respect of describing it. It was just crap and expensive crap. We'll try again tomorrow, I jest! Bed at 10:30 pm. Off on Kuranda sky rail to Kuranda. If you can make sense of that, please explain it to me, and I'm going there. (I must remember to take my johnnies).

Just to clarify – johnnies – St John's Wort… ha

Tuesday, 12ᵗʰ January

Up at 7 am - coach (luxury Melba says) to Kuranda. Leaving at 8:40 am. What a fantastic day. Coach up Kennedy highway (an Englishman who was a very, very silly man who tried to reach Kuranda from Cairns somewhere in the mid-1800s - died 8 years after arriving in Australia and in the process killed all but 3 of his 50-man team together with his sheep (should have been cows for such a hazardous journey through a mountain rain forest). In 1905 a local man and his son with a plough and a bulldozer won the contract to build the road (a single-lane road), which they did successfully on budget under time. This road up a mountain is 7.5 km long. Anyways I digress; when we reached Kuranda (derived from the aboriginal name for the Flax or stream Lily), we fiddled around for a few hours. Melba visited a butterfly sanctuary, I didn't because I've seen butterflies. We had a light lunch followed by the piece de resistance: The sky rail 7.5k metres long above a rainforest 250 metres below, breathtaking. 2 intermediate stops where one hops off the gondolas to pre-organised lookouts over the Barron gorge and river. It should be classified as one of the wonders of the world, and yet it was only constructed four years ago. Took eight months to build, 7 ½ years to plan. It was all constructed from Russian helicopters and only cost 8 million Australian dollars, absolute peanuts.

Back at hotel by 4 pm – swim, write up log together with a few cards. Lunch tonight in the bar pool cage. Menu looks good, and I've already sampled the excellent wine. I've just realised that this is our last night in Australia. We spent it in the Cafe Royale, sounds flash but read for this pool café. Super meal. Antipasti (everything imaginable. including tripe - Melba had mine) together with a plate of fish, chicken, mussels, prawns, etc, all in light beer batter. We shared both plates - we're not big eaters, accompanied by chardonnay, water, gin, and brandy, and coffee.

Bed at 10 pm after a big of telly and a read of the international "Daily Mail" dated 11th Jan and covering the previous week. Surprised to read that we have gained victory over Japan (I thought it was the 15th of August). Just filled in questionnaire for hotel and gave restaurant Colossus - 2/10. everything else 'Excellent'.

https://www.skyrail.com.au

Wednesday, 13th January 1999

Awake at 7 am, we're packed and ready to leave hotel for Cairns airport to board flight SO240 leaving at 11:30 am for Singapore (we're informed that the flight should be maximum 5 hours - we'll see!) It's bloody amazing, last night, I mentioned India on some cards we were sending home, and by 11:30, I had the runs. I've spent all night writing in pain or/and sitting on the toilet chewing Diocalm tablets. It's nearly 7 am, and I've still got it, and I'm flying in a few hours. Oh my god!

Thursday, 14th January

Awake at 7 am. The period between 7 am yesterday and now has been a nightmare. Somehow got through the flight 6 ½ hours eventually arrived at Hotel Boulevard (Orchard Road) Singapore at 4:30 pm. Went straight to bed and just woken up. Feeling better but weak and slightly nauseous. Melba has just presented me with two malaria tablets. I do not believe it!

At 8:30 am, we're getting on a bus to tour Singapore - yippee! I did this yesterday coming from the airport - I would describe Singapore as big, high, wide, and clean, plus millions of trees, end of story. Still Thursday 14th January time 12:30. Back at the hotel. I've been on a bus and seen places but do not feel up to writing about it, so I'm afraid, dear reader, it's over to the "cub".

On the coach passed 'scandal point' near St Andrews cathedral where the British used to meet in the park all dressed in their finery to gossip about this and that, after which they would go to Raffles for drinks and dinner. Went by the Singapore river through city of lions =Singapore. Saw the Raffles hotel. Stamford Raffles founded Singapore. 640 square km is Singapore, the temperature is 25- 35 degrees every day of the year and has 240 days of rain! The old fish market now consists of 50-60 stalls, all serving different foods. Good place to sample all the local delicacies. We then went to Chinatown and saw the Sri Mariamman Temple, which is a national monument. Singapore has 3.1 million people (3000 per sq. km!). In the first week of November every year, everyone plants a tree. Then on to faber point, which is a "lookout spot" over the sea and sky rail to a little holiday island for the locals. The island was called Sentosa (peace and tranquillity). We then visited a gem factory and saw them carving jade and many other precious stones. Our final visit was to the botanical gardens, which has an orchid area containing over 800 different types of orchids.

Not bad for a 'cub' but for those amongst you who are interested in the indigenous facts. I suggest you pay a visit to your local library.

https://www.millenniumhotels.com/en/singapore/orchard-hotel-singapore

ACTUAL FLYING TIME TO DATE: 45 ¾ HOURS

A note for the "Lancet" St John's wort (formally known as johnnies) do not work either in Singapore or when one is feeling ill.

The Hotel Boulevard on Orchard St is superb. Open-air swimming pools on both the 8th and 3rd floor. Super restaurant, boutiques, nightclubs. etc. wonderful service, the cub says. I love to say wonderful food, not just restaurant. It's now 7 pm, and I can feel the lifeblood beginning to flow. I hope it's not a false alarm.

Random thought - Singapore Airport is massive but so big and airy that one doesn't feel oppressed.

Friday, 15th January

Awake at 7 am feeling tons better, good job as were off to India tonight, leaving this hotel at 6 pm. here's a fact for you even though not verifiable in a library, true all the same. For a 2-night stay in Singapore, I have slept in this bed for 28 hours.

Shortly after a light breakfast, we shall be off down the famous Orchard Road to shop until Melba drops. Had breakfast at the LA TERRASSE DE DELIFRANCE in the sunshine on Orchard Street. Melba asked the waiter where Mohammed Mustafa and son was - not unlike asking someone in Woking where J. Brown and son was without mentioning newsagents or West End, Chobham. Not surprisingly, he didn't know, especially as he was an immigrant Indian. We eventually found the Mustafa centre in Little India, 2 minutes from the Hindu temple, which the cab referred to yesterday. This was a lovely intro. As the real thing, the sounds, the smell of spices, and the 'gobbing' in the streets. I'm not sure if they get points for hitting one's shoes, but there were some very close calls. I shall have to get in a bit of practice for tomorrow.

Our plane SQ412 (Singapore Airlines) leaves from Changi @ 8-45pm and arrives at 24:00 hrs in Mumbai (Bombay to you and me). This does not indicate 3 ¼ hour flight due to time changes. So will have to see. Note hardly any crime, but we never saw one policeman in the whole time in Singapore.

Saturday, 16ᵗʰ January

It's 1:40 am local time, and we've just arrived at out hotel Ramada Palm Grove Bombay. The flight was very pleasant and only took 5 hours.

ACTUAL FLYING TIME TO DATE: 50 ¾ HOURS

However, from 11:30 local time until now has been a nightmare-first we queued for 1 ½ hours just to get through customs. Mumbai airport is seething mass of bodies in a very dilapidated small area. Then because of the time in the queue, our luggage had been taken off the carousel and spread around everywhere. Once we contacted our agent (from Pettit's), we waited a further ½ hour for our transport to make its way from the incredibly congested car park all unmade. Our transport, ha! - A converted van with curtains and a temple in front that flashed red and green lights. The driver was a maniac. On my life, I didn't think we would make it. He overtook inside, outside, went through umpteen red lights whilst at the same time rolling from right to left. Even though it was dark, it looked like driving through the most dusty run-down area imaginable but hey, what a surprise the hotel is like a flower in a briar patch. Very Indian, just as I imagined, but smart with it. We're being picked up later at 9-00 for our first leg of the journey to Varanasi by plane - God help us.

ACTUAL FLYING TIME TO DATE: 52 ¾ HOURS

We get to the Bombay airport somehow, same driver (he'd now been working all night). The domestic airport is chaotic, but with help, we're now awaiting our flight. Weather 31 degrees but haven't experienced it due to 'taxi' (ha) and airport. Bombay by day is one experience, a quite incredible place. Beggars, cripples, and also there are the top echelon of society here. I suppose some people would call it exciting. I prefer frightening. I actually feel like Michael Palin. Melba is Passepartout. Flight no. Sahara airways S2907 leaving at 10:35 am arriving 12:35 am (a man has just gobbed in the ashtray immediately in front of me). We've been sitting in the wrong section for 40 mins, but still, we've found the right area now, and the plane is still not boarding (no explanation). It's due to fly at 10:35 am, and it's 10:40 am now. Oh, the joys of being a travelling man. The sun looks lovely through the window.

Here in Varanasi (the holy city) (3:00 pm) at the Hotel Taj Ganges and what a fantastic hotel. Imagine the days of the Raj. It is simply magnificent. It says in front of me, "the most unique Sanskrit saying means quite simply a guest must be treated as God." We've cancelled this afternoon's car ride with guide to see a few temples in order to enjoy the hotel and rest for a while. Temperature here is 12 degrees (twelve) but clear and sunny. The hired car for the rest of our holiday is a proper hire car (an ambassador), but the drivers are the same as in Bombay; they drive continuously on their car horns. This clears the way through the bicycles, Rickshaws, 2-wheel taxis and cows... and, of course, people. The whole area is covered in dust. Buildings range from part tile, part brick (no mortar), tin and wood (this described the best buildings) to mud and hay with plastic. The houses lined the road for 22 km from the little airport to the hotel area, with people either sitting around or praying in the land between buildings. The Cub has begrudgingly agreed to finish the log for today. One last word today from your moving reporter - Melba is now wearing my chinos because she cannot fit into her own jeans or long white trousers!

Went down to have pre-dinner drinks. Raymond had a gin fizz, and I had Cinzano and tonic - I don't know what it was, but it didn't taste like Cinzano! We had a very nice buffet with plenty of choices - mostly Indian, very enjoyable, especially as we were serenaded by an Indian dressed in national costume and playing a type of sitar - very good to start with, but very repetitive. 9 pm. Off to bed now, as we have to be up at 6:15 am to see the sun rise over the Ganges.

The meal - imagine all the choices on the best Indian restaurant menu but eaten in an authentic ambiance, and then you've got it.

https://www.tajhotels.com/en-in/taj/taj-ganges

Sunday, 17th January

Up at 6 am driver and guide took us on tour of Varanasi - unfortunately, it was bloody freezing fog. What is even worse, Kool, our guide, tells us that all the areas we shall be visiting until we go back to Bombay in 9 days' time will be subject to fog and temperature around 5 degrees. Without the guide and chauffeured Mercedes, it would be impossible to move in Varanasi because of all the beggars, pedlars, and deformed cripples surrounding oneself.

We went first to the banks of the sacred river Ganges where thousands of lunatics bathed in the Ganges, praying constantly. The holy men sat on the banks (they're not stupid) and provide mirrors and combs for the lunatics when they came out of the water. They also smacked various coloured paint made from sandalwood and God knows what else on their faces after they'd donned their dry-ish rags. The loonies then climbed hundreds of steps up to their respective places of worship. Next stop, would you believe an electric burning house for those presumably who caught pneumonia and died. Very cheap, we were told only 200 rupees (£3) whereas a funeral pyre can cost you 1500 rupees. We saw one show, local boy, I think, and then saw his family (usually eldest son) putting his ashes and bones, if he hadn't burnt well, into a basket which he then emptied into the river Ganges. The smell pervading the whole area was rather unpleasant! We saw and had explained the place (Sarnath) where Buddha first preached his message of enlightenment 2500 years ago. The poverty and sickness have to be seen to be understood.

Numerous temples, universities, stupas were visited (see Pettitt's India Tour).

It's now 1:30 pm. Still foggy, and nothing to do except read in the lounge. And have coffee; alcohol isn't really an option here. On a lighter note, we also visited a place where three little wizened old men made beautiful raw silk and gold thread saris, scarves, tapestries, and cushion covers, on incredibly intricate looms, naturally, all hand moved, no electric or mechanical parts. The three men produce 3 x 45 inches per day. We also went to see some carpets up to 1200 knots per square inch. P.S. Jackie Onassis had lots of gear from the silk place. Her photo taken in the shop was proudly portrayed, no doubt mine will be hung there as from tomorrow. 4 pm, We've just returned to our room after having a snack in the Mandap restaurant within the hotel (one can't really go out of the grounds alone). We thought we had ordered a samosa each; imagine our surprise when we were served a dosa something or other approx. 18" long containing spiced potatoes and onions together with a bowl of mulligatawny soup each, followed by a samosa containing meat the size of each being 10"x10". After consuming all this, including two bowls of mulligatawny soup (very, very spicy), we found out it was actually curry sauce. We've decided that we're not capable of entering the restaurant again other than for breakfast and then only choosing eggs and toast.

That's it for today; our guide Kool is collecting us at 9:30 am tomorrow morning for another trip to the river of death, where he hopes we will be able to get on a rowing boat and watch a funeral pyre in progress. I tell you, it's a laugh a minute here.

Monday, 18th Jan

Awake at 6:30 am it's now 11:30 am, and we've had a superb tour of the city on foot through streets 6'0" wide lined with bazaars selling spices, silks, perfumes, etc. We also saw the golden temple next to a very heavily guarded (barbed wire, steel posts, and soldiers) mosque, all due to historical reasons. The streets are teeming with people, animals, and scooters. Monkeys abound around the temple.

We went on a rowing boat up and down the Ganges seeing all the ghats (steps) leading up to numerous temples at the bottom of which the lunatics were bathing and washing clothes. We saw a cremation in progress, the body floating on the edge of the Ganges whilst the family built the bonfire. Several dead animals floated together, with river dolphins leaping out of the water. The main cremation ground, surprisingly, is owned by an untouchable, probably the richest man in Varanasi.

Our new young guide for the day, name unknown, was terrific. Last year he guided Jack Straw, wife, and both children around the same areas he took us. He knew all about the son and his drug charges.

The local people are incredibly philosophical. For example, whilst grandma burns on her pyre, there are no tears, the children play cricket within a few yards of the pyre. They consider life to be a preparation for death. Children (babies) and holy men are not burnt but just dumped in the river weighted with a stone. I know this all makes grim reading, but the reality is one of joy and peace of mind. Example - unbelievable traffic chaos but absolutely no road rage or anything resembling it, everybody accepts. Wouldn't it be great if we could all be like this. I'm getting there because we've just been told that our flight to Khajuraho is delayed from 1:30 pm to 5 pm (maybe), and I don't care! The flight is now delayed for a further hour and may be cancelled altogether - the peace of mind is quickly evaporating - I'm now pissed off! Sitting around the pool with jumpers and jackets on, two very large eagles (or vultures) alighted on some chair backs about 5 yards from where we were sitting. They were vultures (just checked in hotel).

At airport now, 5 pm told flight arrives at 6:30 pm departure. Local agent superb; he's waiting until we actually go thru security (if we do). Chaos reigns. 8:20 pm, and here we are in our Hotel Chandela in Khajuraho and a beautiful hotel it is part of the TAJ group, same as the last hotel. We're off down to dinner now - Toodledoo. Very nice - Hong Kong style chicken in garlic sauce with egg rice; Melba, Macaroni bolognese, bed at 10:30 pm.

https://chandela.in

ACTUAL FLYING TIME TO DATE: 53 ½ HOURS

Tuesday, 19th January

Awake at 7 am. Today we're off to tour the eastern and western group of temples and to study the erotic carvings of the Kama Sutra. Therefore, this afternoon will be spent in our bedroom practicing the techniques. Actually, our agent here is trying to get us to pay for an extra trip in a jeep to see some waterfall and animals, but we've decided to give him the elbow and his dancing girl show tonight. The weather is fog which I'm told will lift by midday. We leave for the temples at 8:30 am.

The West Temples, 1000 years old, are Hindu temples. The Kama Sutra was written before this period. The last four layers of incredible carvings in sandstone around the Cuppola depict Erotica (see postcards). Without a guide, all one would see would be the obvious carvings of either men giving women one from many positions or men being given blow jobs, or maybe the odd woman masturbating, but with the guide, he points out all the subtleties of other carvings. The Eastern temples are less than 1000 years because they represent the Jains, a breakaway group who were into peace and tranquillity and didn't agree with Erotica. These carvings were a drag. No, they were also incredible, but no naughties.

From 11 am, the sun came out, thank God, so in the afternoon, we sat around the pool and had one beer between us. Temperature about 18 degrees. That's it for today, folks, evening meal, tv, and bed.

Wednesday, 20th January

Awake at 7 am. Today we drove with our driver to Jhansi for the train to Agra, stopping on the way at Orchha (another holy city). A resort mainly where the Indian government ministers come for holidays. They fly by helicopter. We travelled 4 hours by car on incredibly bad roads; however, I'm beginning to understand the driving. One drives in the middle and leans on the horn the whole time, especially thru villages. When you see Melba's picture of Orchha, visualize the river full of rocks, 30 feet higher, during the monsoon period of July and August.

N.B: Cow pats for cooking.

Ramsing (Maharaja) temples are at Orchha. Muslim temple - Sheesh Mahal at Orchhra. Arrived at Jhansi - Pettit's office at 5 pm to be told that the Shatabi express train was delayed and wouldn't arrive till 7 pm; therefore, our driver would take us to an Indian hotel for coffee and stay here until six then return to his office for a move to the station. All very unsettling. Melba is not looking happy. C'est la vie as we say in India. We asked our driver how old his ambassador car was, like a flash, he said four years. The lying bastard, it has to be minimum 20 years old. Believe me. See picture of porter carrying all our cases. 2 small boys had fun whilst we waited on the platform for the train by throwing live rats at us from across the line. Great fun! To top it all, the lights went out on the platform - it was pitch black; imagine Melba's face - she is not a happy bunny. The train journey is not very nice. We're surrounded by our luggage and cannot move for the next 2 ½ hours until we get to Agra. It's now 11:45 pm, and after fighting to get 3 cases off the train whilst people were trying to board with their luggage, we have arrived at the Trident hotel in Agra. And very, very nice it is too. We decide to have chicken burgers and chips with a pot of coffee in our room, delicious. Now it's Bo bo's after a very long day. Melba is now smiling she made it.

https://www.tridenthotels.com/hotels-in-agra

Thursday, 21st January

Awake at 6 am and raring to go. Today we leave at 10 am for our tour of Agra to see the Agra fort on the banks of the Yamuna River, followed by the Taj Mahal. Including the tomb of I'timad-ud-Daula, the jewel of Agra. Whole building covered in white marble and semi-precious stones. 9:30 fog doesn't seem to be lifting.

Note: all the travellers to India need to be strong and resilient. 2:15 pm - lunch at the Trident. (Equivalent of chicken tikka). Brilliant morning -Baby Taj and Agra Fort. Superb, guide-knowledgeable, helpful, and pleasant. Visited jewellers, so it's over to the cub.

We have seen the most beautiful embroidery pictures dotted with real gemstones that one could ever see. All with 3D effect. Then on to jewellery. Melba tried on a priceless emerald and diamond ring which was (part of the original crown of the queen mahal) fantastic. Raymond decides I could have it for my birthday. Only joking! Actually, he has bought me a beautiful ring (emerald and diamonds). The jeweller is bringing it to the hotel tonight as it needed to be made smaller. Who's a lucky girl, then!

This afternoon now that the sun is shining, we shall visit the Taj Mahal itself - what an incredible place it is. The symmetry is incredible to think in the 16th century; they could build in such marvellous perspectives where for 200 yards, everything is in line to something like 1/100th of an inch and the reflections in the water. Wherever you look, there are either 4 of everything or 2 of everything. Identical to the most minute detail. Also, the overall size of the

Mausoleum (because that is what it is) is so big, something that tv and photos do not reveal. Melba bought an example of the type of marble and precious stone inlay. The guide 'Rishi' was even good enough to barter on Melba's behalf for the presents she bought.

Dinner and collect and pay for ring (when jeweller arrives at hotel) then tv and bed. Ready for our next move to Ranthambore Tiger Reserve, stopping on way at Fatehpur Sikri – a deserted red stone city built by Emperor Akhbar in the 16th century. Tomorrow's journey is expected to take up to 7 hours before we reach the lodge.

Friday, 22nd January

Awake at 7:30 am. Last minute packing once again, breakfast, settle hotel bill, and we're back on the road at 9:30 am. Note: Basil and tea boil drink - good for sore throat.

A day's journey in a car doesn't sound good but believe me, the sights and sounds, and smells we experienced will live with us forever. Weather today about 22c. Camels, water buffalo, monkeys, sheep, Goats, Sheep, Donkeys, Cows, Pigs, Peacocks, Vultures, we saw them all along the way to Ranthambore (Rajasthan).

Notes: Police robbery joke - 12 hrs before.

Saw women making rope from raw materials.

5:30 pm, and here we are in the 'Lodge' at Ranthambore. It's very difficult for me, dear reader, to describe the incongruity of this place. First, the lodge was built, God knows when, as a hunting lodge for the Maharaja of Jaipur. It is, in fact, now a hotel with modern facilities but with an ambience of old India. The more difficult part is to describe its location. We have travelled for 6 hours since leaving Fatehpur Sikri on mostly unmade roads; the surrounding areas have either been fields of mustard or wheat or completely arid areas with goat and sheep roaming around. We came through numerous villages, which all looked like gypsy encampments even though there were shops and houses of sorts. The villages are all strewn with rubbish and litter, people urinate everywhere, and dust covers everything. Still, this is India, and we came to see it. As we came through each village, everybody craned their heads to look at us, and the children, in particular, gave us big wide smiles and waved at us. Melba sat in the car like the queen giving it the royal wave. They were obviously delighted to see us. Apparently, "English bastard" is a sign of endearment, I'm told. 7:30 pm, dinner - can't wait. Sorry, the full name of the lodge is Sawai Madhapur Lodge. Set-dinner buffet (chicken Jalfrezi, pork, etc, etc). One is not supposed to eat pork for health reasons. What do I do? - had them both, so fingers crossed. I'm currently listening to 2 prats - Doctor and Lawyer and they are talking crap – loudly. Oh, by the way, the Queen and Prince Phillip stayed here in 1961. I hope they had a better coffee than I'm drinking. Must go to Bo bo's now; got to be up at 6 am tomorrow - safari by jeep starts at 7 am in the reserve, we're hoping to see Tigers.

https://www.seleqtionshotels.com/en-in/sawai-madhopur-lodge

Saturday, 23rd January (Melba's birthday)

I haven't got a card, but at least I bought her a present, and I can sing. Up at 6 am. Breakfast at 6:15 am in jeep at 7:00 am, and off to the tiger reserve we go. 11:00 am, and we've spent the last 3 ½ hours in the jungle and not seen one poxy tiger, leopard, or cheetah. We saw lots of Antelope, Crocodiles, Monkeys, and many, many birds. The highlight was 2 Sloth bears but seen from about ½ mile away through binoculars. The sun is now out but hazy, pleasant. Lunch will be served at about 1 pm on the lawn, and then it's back to the jungle for another 3 ½ hours. 6:45 pm. Just showered. Got back from the jungle at 5:45 pm- nothing - even worse than this morning - in future, I'll stick to zoos. Spoke to a young Jewish woman lawyer who works for Warner Brothers. I told her I thought LA was the pits. She was born and lives in LA. I know how to make friends. I was glad to get away from her; what a bore, she must wear a mouth out each day. Just been told the Maharani of Jaipur was here for three days last week (she's 80 years old and very active - lives in Jaipur, London, etc); rich bitch. Tonight, dinner was served outside in a courtyard, it was dark and very cold, but they surrounded us with logs, fires and laid on an Indian puppet show together with a man who sang and played a bongo. I have vision of the fado singer at the Fortaleza Praia de luz. It's only 8:30 pm, but we're going to bed to read - just hope this stupid Indian man packs up his singing and smacking his bongo soon because it's right next to our lodge (a sort of Indian chalet).

Sunday, 24th January

Awake at 7:30 am - leisurely breakfast, and then were off to Jaipur by road, 3 ½ hours of crap road (yes, I am taking the St John's wort).

Arrived at Jaipur - Hotel Trident at 1:30 pm. Superb hotel - the best. Feeling tired and in need of Sun. Booked in and retired to poolside loungers, ordered chicken tikka and a couple of beers - very relaxed - unfortunately, the bloody clouds covered the sun at 3:15 pm. What a bummer. So, we've retired to our beautiful room for coffee and to write up the log, after which we shall stroll around the superb gardens and look over the massive lake to somebody or others palace. Jaipur is the first reasonably civilized city we've seen, but don't get carried away; there's still people living all over the streets and animals roaming everywhere, plus the incredible noise of the traffic - bicycle rickshaws, auto rickshaws, etc etc. Dinner tonight in the Jalmahal (the water palace) restaurant, after pre-dinner drinks in the Mansagar bar. Flying homemade kites is very big in India... and having babies. I'm not sure if there is a connection. 8:30 pm - Melba is aghast! One double G+T /and 1 Cinzano + 7up, a buffet each, and one beer and one water and coffee (N.B buffet plentiful and various - delicious), cost 2000 rupees, nearly 30 pounds. In the past, 1000 rupees. I'm changing my nickname from Ray the £5 to Ray the 1000Rupees.

Tv and bed. Tomorrow is the Amber Fort (10 minutes away), travelling up to it by Elephant. We've decided to cancel the afternoon tour of the city as we virtually did that on the way here. So hopefully, the sun will shine, and I shall have a swim in the pool and relax.

https://www.tridenthotels.com/hotels-in-jaipur

https://www.jaipurstuff.com/jal-mahal-jaipur

Monday, 25th January

Awake at 7 am for some unknown reason, we both slept fitfully. Weather looks good; just seen sunrise over mountains. A beautiful hot sunny day. We left for the amber fort at 9 am. By 9:15 am, we were sitting on our elephant with the mahout going up the long winding hill to the fort and palace. Absolutely breath-taking. After an hour, we descended by jeep and surprised our guide and driver by asking to be taken back to the hotel. The guide obviously wanted to take us to see the pink city and go to manufacturers of gems, pottery, and textiles. Where I'm told they receive 40% of all sale. So tough luck to him. We spent the rest of the day swimming and reading, including lunch around the pool set in magnificent surrounding. Dinner in Jal mahal, tv, and Bo Bo's. We have to leave the hotel at 7 am for our flight from Jaipur to Mumbai at 8:35 am. Note: at the Amber Fort (see postcard), the painting on the wall is called Ganesh and is made from semi-precious ground stones mixed with cow's dung and urine. Bear in mind the painting has remained intact over 300 years, open to all the elements. Incredible.

NUMBER OF HOTELS TO DATE 14 + NESSA'S

Tuesday, 26th January

Awake at 6 am. Car to Jaipur airport leaves hotel at 7 am. 7:30 am, and here we are at Jaipur airport. Very smart marble floor, recognisable shops, etc. Our agent has done everything for us - booked us in, passed our luggage through, and is waiting with us for our flight to be called. The flight is Jet Airways 9W-374. Flight 1 ½ hours.

ACTUAL FLYING TIME TO DATE: 55 HOURS

Here we are at the Ramada Palm Grove Hotel - same place we stayed for a few hours when coming from Singapore. The hotel is much better than we thought - lovely pool, roof, sunbathing garden, etc. Temperature here in Bombay - in the 30s. Arrived here at 10:30 am at 2:30 pm, we're off on a tour of Bombay.

26th January is Republic Day. The day Britain gave up power and handed it to the Indians - so we're very popular as you can imagine - "British Colonial Bastards", they cry as we drive through the city, waving like the Queen's mother, occasionally running over a one-legged leper who mistimed his begging mission. Note: because today is a national holiday - alcohol is banned, but we're English, so Ner ner ner ner ner!

6:00 pm just back from a great tour of Bombay, except for the traffic; how more people are not killed, I do not know. We visited Gandhi's house (very, very awe-inspiring), the Hanging Gardens (so-called because they are built OVER a reservoir. The hill upon which dead people of the Persis sect are placed for vultures to eat the bodies (takes between 6-8 hours), and then the remaining bones are put down a well filled with lime. This is all because the Persis (from Persia) do not believe in contaminating the air, water, or ground.

We also visited the Gateway of India, Malabar Hill, where beautiful Victorian-style buildings, built by the British in the late 18th - early 19th century, are lived in by the upper middle classes - prices comparable to London. Many of the British-built buildings are out of this world and are still in use as universities, museums, railway stations, and police stations. We also visited the famous LAUNDRY, an outdoor laundry covering two football pitch-sized areas. Unbelievable, and this isn't for the poor; this is where the middle and upper middle class have their laundry done. Finally, we saw Chowpatty Beach. Swimming in the Arabian sea around Bombay is out because we were told it is polluted for up to 9 miles offshore. Tonight, it's drinkies, dinner, tv, and bed. Tomorrow the car and driver are ours to do as we wish.

Fantastic food, best selection in India. Had discussion with manager who felt that the British left 30 years too soon; he wishes we were still ruling India to bring some organisation to the country and enable the people to grow as opposed to the ignorant, corrupt ministers who currently rule India. Note: our guide in Varanasi, it would appear, was a fundamentalist, i.e., a naughty man hence his comment on Gandhi and the caste system he wanted re-instated. Note: The Tata group seem to control India, steel, cars, construction, consultancy, tea, soap, etc., etc. (the Tata family are Persis (bodies eaten by vultures). Apparently, they are highly regarded people, especially by the British during the days of the Raj. - clever, honest, hardworking, reliable. Only 40,000 left in India and a dying race, as they won't involve themselves in intermarriage.

https://www.wyndhamhotels.com/en-uk/ramada/juhu-mumbai-india/ramada-plaza-palm-grove/overview

Wednesday, 27th January

Awake at 7:30 am after a very bad night's sleep for no obvious reason. At 9:30 am, with the car and driver at our disposal all day, we had decided to go to Sanjay Gandhi National Park to go on yet another safari in the hope of seeing a tiger on the 3rd attempt. We hope to be back at 12:00 pm in order to spend the afternoon around the pool, reading, swimming, and soaking up the sun. We got back at 1 pm due to our stupid driver who drove through a jungle, then a temple, which we didn't want to see. One finds that one can over-face oneself with Temples.

Now, the Safari. First, we had to pay for a whole Bus to take us into the Safari-Tiger area. All of 220 rupees (£3), then 7 or 8 people jumped on our Bus. Saw nothing until the driver pepped his horn and then let the tiger out of his cage into the jungle. It walked eventually in front of the bus for about 100 yards, found its swimming pool, and crawled in. We also saw one other Tiger about 50 yards away, this time a White Tiger (or a Bengal Tiger with a sheet over itself). The afternoon was idyllic; swimming, reading, a couple of beers (kingfishers), a look over the beach from the rooftop garden, then a bite to eat before going back to read around the pool. Weather hot sun but Bombay suffers badly from smog. When one sees the number of crap vehicles, it is no wonder India's population is 900 million! All congregated into a few cities and villages.

6 pm and we are fast approaching the end of an epic journey (oh! hasn't he got a lovely turn of phrase). All that's left now is our last dinner in India, plus another frantic car ride thru Bombay to the airport. We're being collected for our flight at 11 pm. The flight - Singapore airline no SQ 328. Leaving at 2:20 am 28/1/99. Here we are at Mumbai airport, and I'm totally pissed off. We arrived here 11:30 am - first, we had no assistance whatsoever from Pettitt's agent. Queued ¾ hour to have baggage passed through security, then waited another 1-hour queue to book in, then waited without seats, then ¾ hr wait in a dismal waiting area without any facilities until we boarded. Our seats were 37 D + E, which meant we boarded last.

*India's population now, at time of publishing, is almost
1.4 billion, and having checked, it was actually 1 billion at
the time of this around-the-world trip, 24 years on therefore,
the population has increased by a whopping 400 million
people!*

Thursday, 28th January (crept in)

Bollocks to India. I've just completed a suggestion form,
so you can imagine my comments. Melba appears calm. The
flight was fortunately very good. 9 ½ hrs arriving about 7:30
am to be met by Carol. One more leg tomorrow, and that's
the end.

ACTUAL FLYING TIME TO DATE: 64 ½ HOURS

Lovely evening dinner at Carol's; nice to see Mandy, Oliver, David, and Barbara. Bed at 1:30 haven't slept since awaking at 7-30am on Wednesday.

Carol is Mum's sister, still lives in Manchester – Oliver & Mandy, Carol's children, my cousins. David was Melba's Mum's second husband, Arthur's son, and his wife Barbara (who I used to fancy as a teenager – never saw that being published anywhere ;)).

Friday, 29th January

Awake at 7 am feeling wide awake, fit and healthy. Back to an airport (runway) this morning.

Left Carol's at 11:am for the 12:35 flight to Heathrow (BA 1393)

ACTUAL FLYING TIME TO DATE: 65 ½ HOURS - OY VEY!

Arrived at Heathrow 1:10 pm; having got bags, we were met by a very excited Jack, Nat, Charlie, and Gemma with a welcome home banner that Jack had made. It was lovely to see them all - it's been so long. Nat drove us back home, and we're back.

What a journey

It was a wonderful adventure for team 'Mum & Dad', indeed, so much so they went on another World trip two years later via Vanessa's in Australia, to be there for the birth of Melba & Raymond's seventh Grandchild (Their 8th and final Grandchild, my daughter Katie, was born 3 years after this trip).

Reading the book brought both Mum & Dad back to life for me. It was lovely to hear their voices in my head. Happy, warm, loving, and laughing voices, living a wonderful journey together. Remembering them from their last few years of life apart, as Mum had to be cared for in a home with Alzheimer's, was not the memory I wanted. I think this 'round the world logbook' portrays them in a much truer and more real way than I could ever write myself, reading their own words and thoughts, travelling together.

Raymond, my dad, died at 81 years old on 17th April 2018 from Septicaemia in the brain, from what was effectively an earache that he didn't get sorted; it was a lesson to learn from. Indeed, many of my life lessons were from either from what my dad did right or did wrong. When I was at school in the seventies, society was full of racists and bigots in the UK, including some uncles and parents of children at school. Dad strongly disagreed with any form of racism and wouldn't keep his thinking to himself but would call racists and racism out whenever he saw it. His own childhood was clearly influenced by living in a very Jewish area of North Manchester, and he found himself in a group of all Jewish youths who would be antisemitically attacked by other gangs of youths; Dad wouldn't ignore and got involved in many scrapes. He always stressed it was ignorance that causes racism. However, it was his inaction and hesitance to ever visit the doctor when something was wrong with him, always thinking it'll go away, that after he died, I decided to check out a little mole on my back (which I would've done nothing about prior to Dad's death). This was an important learning, as it was instantly diagnosed as a melanoma, and left untreated would've introduced cancer to many other parts of my body.

Melba, my mum, died at 85years old on 18th January 2022, 5 days before her 86th Birthday, after approximately nine years of Alzheimer's, which, as is the case, got progressively worse, particularly through the Covid years, when she could no longer speak any sense. She forgot my name about three years before she died but would call me her 'special friend' and always used the words 'family' and 'I love you' until the day her speech went completely. She was an incredibly beautiful woman, inside and out. Always smiling. Her encouragement for me to study ensured I went to university. I had not been a great student up until the age of 9; in fact, it was seeing my Mum crying after reading a poor school report that made me buckle down at school and made sure I was top or close to top of class for everything, to make her happy. I have always had a lifelong love of learning since then, and continued to study throughout my life, including currently studying for a master's degree in Archaeology at UCL now, at the young age of 60.

ALL PROCEEDS FROM THIS BOOK WILL BE GIVEN TO THE ALZHEIMERS SOCIETY www.alzheimers.org.uk

The last ever picture of the Flynn family all together was taken at a restaurant in Chobham, Surrey, Mum's favourite…Vanessa was over in the UK from Australia, so we had Mum, Dad, me, Natalie & Vanessa. Lily J (was initially Gemma, but her name swapped to her second name at a very early age), Holly & Amanda too. The restaurant had been a Flynn Family regular 'special' over the years – mainly as 'The Four Seasons', then later as 'Mei'. Mum had her 60th birthday party there, with so many of my parents' friends and relations. I had my 21st Birthday dinner there with Amanda, my university girlfriend at the time, and a very sunburnt sister Natalie with Mum & Dad. We would have many 'special' family dinners there. Katerina was also nicknamed 'Snow white' there by Alma, Uncle Keith's wife

(Keith present in Mum & Dad's wedding photo on page V)

13th October 2016

Printed in Great Britain
by Amazon

18360039R00068